RUN, LEAP, SAIL, DUNK

Run, Leap, Sail, Dunk

A Collection of Stories from a Sports-Crazy Father

Venkat Srinivasan

To Appa and Amma

And...

*To Gregg Popovich and Tim Duncan
for rekindling my faith in sports*

A Parent Talks to a Child
Before the First Game

This is your first game, my child. I hope you win.
I hope you win for your sake, not mine.
Because winning's nice.
It's a good feeling.
Like the whole world is yours.
But, it passes, this feeling.
And what lasts is what you've learned.

And what you learn about is life.
That is what sports is all about. Life.
The whole thing is played out in an afternoon.
The happiness of life.
The miseries.
The joys.
The heartbreaks.

There's no telling what'll turn up.
There's no telling whether they'll toss you out in the first
*   five minutes, or whether you'll stay for the long haul.*

There's no telling how you'll do.
You might be a hero or you might be absolutely nothing.
There's just no telling.
Too much depends on chance.
On how the ball bounces.

I'm not talking about the game, my child.
I'm talking about life.

But, it's life that the game is all about.
Just as I said.

Because every game is life.
And life is a game.
A serious game.
Dead Serious.

But, that's what you do with serious things.
You do your best.
You take what comes.
You take what comes.
And you run with it.

Winning is fun.
Sure.
But winning is not the point.

Wanting to win is the point.
Not giving up is the point.
Never being satisfied with what you've done is the point.
Never letting up is the point.
Never letting anyone down is the point.

Play to win.
Sure.
But lose like a champion.
Because it's not winning that counts.
What counts is trying.

— Author Unknown

Contents

Run, Leap, Sail, Dunk

THE CHAMPION WHO LOOKED BACK (TWICE)

Don't ever underestimate the heart of a champion.

— Rudy Tomjanovich

Buzz Aldrin is not as well known as Neil Armstrong, Tenzing Norgay not as well as Sir Edmund Hillary, the Buffalo Bills certainly not as well as the Dallas Cowboys. Not many people care about or remember who was second. The winner is eulogized as a champion; the second person leads the also-rans.

John Landy, the world record holder from Australia, was perennially being cast as the second-best in the public eye. He had run the race of his life at Turku, Finland, on the 21st of June, 1954. It was a world record time for the mile at 3 minutes and 58 seconds.[1] He had broken the mythical 4-minute barrier for the mile race. However, he was late to the party by 46 days. The British medical student and runner, Roger Bannister, had been the first to run the sub-4-minute mile,[2] and would eventually get knighted for this accomplishment.

A statue of John Landy was later unveiled in Vancouver, British Columbia, but even that was to commemorate a race in which he came second. The mile race at the 1954 Empire Games (in which the member nations of the British Commonwealth, including the United Kingdom, Canada, Australia, and several other countries competed) was dubbed "the Mile of the Century".[3] The showdown between Roger Bannister and John Landy captivated the entire world.

This was a time when track and field was as popular, if not more so, than tennis, golf, boxing, football, or cricket. Sports Illustrated had sent its best correspondent and photographer to cover the event for its first ever issue. The Canadian Broadcasting Company did not have the relay towers to transmit the

TV signals from coast-to-coast. NBC studios, which had the US telecasting rights, had to erect transmitting towers from Vancouver to Seattle from where the signals could be sent across the entire country, even though the United States was not participating in the games. This was the first sporting event to be televised across all of North America. An estimated 100 million people were expected to watch the race, the highlight of the entire games.[4]

The two runners had two distinct approaches to running. John ran against the clock. His only goal was to reach the finish line as fast as he could. He would run at a blistering speed which no one else could keep pace with. Roger Bannister, the budding neurologist, was the tactical runner. He ran against the field. He played the waiting game in a race, keeping within striking distance of the leader. He had a phenomenal finishing kick, which he unleashed at the right moment to leave everybody in the dust.

On the eve of the race, John was jogging barefoot on the grass to try to relax. He suddenly felt a sharp stab of pain. He had stepped on a photographer's broken flashbulb. A two-inch long gash opened up on his foot, from which he was bleeding profusely. He had to get the wound sutured at the hospital. John ensured that this information was not made public.[5]

The next day, John was leading the race, as usual, entering the last lap. He was running hard to stay in front. In the last lap, Roger Bannister started his move. At the last turn of the lap, John looked over his left shoulder to see if Roger had caught up with him. At that precise moment, Roger Bannister ran past him on his right. Try as hard as he did, John could not summon an extra burst of speed to take back the lead. Roger Bannister had won "the Mile of the Century". Both the runners had run the mile in less than four minutes. Roger Bannister had not beaten Landy's world record. But those were mere footnotes. It was not that John had won silver; he had lost gold.[6]

But for the piece of glass that lacerated his foot, history might have been written differently. History is not, however, made of "what-ifs?". John, to his credit, never offered the injury as an excuse. He maintained that he had lost the race fair and square, stating, "I was 100 per cent fit when I entered the race."[7]

"When Landy lost in Vancouver, the whole of Australia cried."[8] John Landy had let an entire nation down. The disappointment and anguish that he felt would have been unfathomable. Here was an athlete who had put his body through a grueling regimen to train himself to be the best in the world. His practice regimen had included running eight to twelve 600-yard laps a day, at a blistering pace, five days a week. On the other days, he would build endurance by running five to seven miles a day.[9] He had sacrificed a lot: several nights of sleep, a chance to fraternize with friends, or have a half-decent social life.

John Landy was emotionally beat. He relived the thoughts of this race for several months. Unfortunately, for sportsmen at the pinnacle of their fields, the defeats remain a painful scar, which are not cured by their victories. It took him more than a year before he was ready to compete in full earnest.

The Australian Championships were being held in John's hometown of Melbourne, at the Olympic Park. John, who had had to endure running in less than optimal conditions in Australia for most of his career, looked forward to running in the newly laid, world-class track. He now had more competition at home. His career had inspired quite a few runners who wanted to follow in his footsteps. Ron Clarke, who would eventually go on to hold most of the distance running records, was one of them.

Over twenty thousand had assembled to witness the race. The crowd was expecting John Landy to break his own world record. The first lap took 59 seconds: world record pace. This time, John was not running in front, but settled in the middle of the pack. They went past the second lap in 2 minutes and 2 seconds. Ron Clarke was running second and John was behind him in third position.[10]

Entering the third lap, the runners were jostling for position.

Suddenly, Ron Clarke tripped. He fell right onto the track.

John was running right behind him. He tried his best to avoid him, but he could not help stepping on Ron Clarke. John's shoes spiked Clarke in his arm.

The rest of the field hurried on. John, however, stopped running. He could not continue. He felt that he had to check on his fallen fellow runner. He turned back.

"Landy...did the most incredible, stupid, beautiful, foolish, gentlemanly act I have ever seen," according to Australian Reverend Gordon Moyes.[11]

He came back to Ron Clarke to find out if he was doing all right. Ron assured him that he was doing fine; he got up, and started to run past John Landy. John had stepped outside the track during his attempt to check on Ron. For a moment, he thought that he had been disqualified.[12] He realized that he was still in the race. The race looked impossible, with the rest of the field ahead by at least 35 yards, if not more.[13] John had lost roughly seven seconds, and had no chance at the World record now. In spite of this, he decided to have a go at the race, and started to run again.

John Landy, the champion runner, was not going to give up. He was in a blind panic, and he didn't think about times or tactics. He just ran. And he ran the only way he knew—as fast as he could. Yard by yard, he was catching up with the leaders. His fellow runners could not keep up with his blistering pace. Entering the final lap, John took the lead. The crowd was cheering wildly. They had never seen a race like this before. History was being enacted in front of their eyes. John, with a great burst of speed, finished the race in first place, almost 12 yards ahead of the next runner. His time: 4:04.2.[14]

The next day, Harry Gordon of the *Sun-News Pictorial*, put so eloquently into words, what the entire stadium might have felt. In an open letter to John Landy, he wrote, "Yours was a classic sporting gesture. It was a senseless piece of chivalry—but it will be remembered as one of the finest actions in the history of sport. In a nutshell, you sacrificed your chance of a world record to go to the aid of a fallen rival. And in pulling up, trotting back to Ron Clarke, muttering

'Sorry' and deciding to chase the field, you achieved much more than any world record...It was your greatest triumph."[15]

A bronze statue was created to commemorate this moment, when John came back to help Ron Clarke, and can be seen even today at the Olympic Park in Melbourne. In 1999, the Sport Australia Hall of Fame voted John Landy's act of sportsmanship the "Finest Sporting Moment of the Century".[16]

Suggested Internet search:
John Landy 1956 Australian Championship race

THE SKYHOOK

*Let me embrace thee, sour adversity, for
wise men say it is the wisest course.*

— William Shakespeare

Magic Johnson, the great point guard of the Los Angeles Lakers, raised his fist as he dribbled the ball. The players, coaches, and even the fans in the stadium knew what that meant. Kareem Abdul-Jabbar was going to get the ball.

Kareem caught the ball and readied himself. He was not facing the basket, but was standing at an angle to it. The defender had to make a choice. If he went up to face him, Kareem would have a clear path to the basket. Kareem would glide by in a flash and dunk the ball. Instead, the defender chose to stand between Kareem and the basket.

Kareem surveyed the landscape. If the defender was overplaying to his right, he could spin to his left and shoot an open jumper. If a double-team came, he was unselfish enough to pass the ball back to Magic, or any other open teammate to take the shot.

Neither was the case: single defender, playing straight up. Kareem planted his left foot and held his left knee straight. He extended his left forearm to ward off the defender. His right arm, which held the ball, went up.[1]

One more decision to make: was the defender jumping to try and block the shot? If so, Kareem would wait until the defender was coming down, and then shoot. No jump. The defender was conceding the shot.

With an aesthetic flick of the wrist, Kareem launched the ball.[2] The flick was the finishing touch. The ball was not propelled towards the basket; it was a father waving goodbye to his kindergarten child at the school's front door.

The hapless defender could only turn around, stare, and hope that the ball would bounce out. No such luck. The ball traversed a smooth arch, and like a homing pigeon, gently landed in the basket. Kareem had scored again with his skyhook.

There has never been a shot so associated with a single player as the skyhook with Kareem Abdul-Jabbar. It is a shot that has a rhythm, a flow and a grace befitting one of the greatest players to ever play the game. The skyhook is considered by many as the "greatest offensive weapon ever unleashed in the NBA."[3] Critics wax poetic of the shot as "the most devastatingly effective, and most beautiful, shot in the history of the game."[4]

In 1961, Lewis Alcindor (as Kareem was known then) arrived at UCLA to join the basketball program under legendary coach, John Wooden, as a much-heralded recruit. Lew, who was 7'1" tall, commanded attention and awe. Even more impressive was his coordination, athleticism, and grace—rare in a seven-footer.

Freshmen were not allowed to represent the University in those days. No problem. In an intra-squad game, Lew led his group of freshmen to victory against the UCLA varsity team, which had won the championship the previous year. These were the lilting and deceptively simple notes of this Beethoven's Führ Elise; the full frontal assault of the violent and yet majestic opening salvo of Symphony No. 5 arrived the next year.

Lew exploded onto the college basketball scene as a sophomore. Fifty-six points in the first game shook and grabbed the college basketball world's attention. In another game, he scored sixty-one points. Here was an unstoppable force. With his height and ability to run and leap, Lewis was a man amongst boys on the basketball floor. Many of his baskets were scored when "he would just turn and dunk," according to his then teammate Gary Cunningham.[5] He scored 29 points and 15.5 rebounds a game, and was named the College Player of the Year.[6] He won every possible, meaningful college accolade. His UCLA team went undefeated and won the National Collegiate Championship.

The NCAA was facing the prospect of two more years of dominance by a single player, so much so that the games were going to be a joke. Spectators were thrilled, but coaches were scared. Short of holding the ball interminably, (this was the pre-shot clock era) there was no way of stopping this one-man wrecking crew.

There was no stopping Lew, once he got the ball close to the basket. Lew could throw down reverse dunks in style, or could take off from just inside the free-throw line and dunk single-handed in one motion. The entire college basketball season would have ended up in a quest to find cannon fodder for UCLA in the finals.

A new rule was enacted. "Basket-stuffing", or what is commonly referred to as dunking, would be outlawed. The official reason from the Rules Committee was that, dunking endangered the safety of the players. Most people felt otherwise. The move was thought to put the brakes on Lew Alcindor. It quickly came to be known as "the Alcindor rule".[7]

Lew chafed at the rule: not because he was worried about his scoring numbers. He was far from a selfish player. If he had wanted to, he could have become the all-time leading scorer in NCAA (National Collegiate Athletic Association) history. But he was willing to sacrifice his scoring for the betterment of the team, much to the appreciation of his coach.[8]

This "no-dunking" rule did not sit well with Lew. He did not buy into the explanation of the Rules Committee. He felt that it was completely unfair that a rule was enacted specifically to prevent him from dominating the game. He even felt that the rule might be racially motivated. He stated that the rule "smacks a little of discrimination. When you look at it...most of the people who dunk are black athletes."[9]

Coach John Wooden, however, concurred with the Rules Committee in outlawing the dunk. He tried to assure Lew that the rule was not made to target him. Eventually, he told him, "It doesn't make any difference whether you are or not [the reason...The rule] is going to make you a better basketball player."[10]

Some skeptics speculated that Lew would not be as great, after the passage of the Lew Alcindor rule. Little did they know of his tremendous desire and determination. Without the ability to dunk the ball now, Lew had to become better at using his other scoring moves. As coach John Wooden recalled, "He worked twice as hard on banking shots off the glass, his little hook across the lane, and his turnaround jumper."[11]

Even as a 5th grader, Lew had experimented with his hook shot.[12] Playing basketball against older children, he had noted that this was a shot that even taller opponents could not block. Now, the hook became a more prominent weapon in his arsenal, as he kept practicing and refining it.

Lew continued to dominate college basketball in spite of the Alcindor rule. He was a consensus All-American in all three years of his eligibility, averaging 26.4 points and 15.5 rebounds a game.[13] His UCLA Bruins won two more national championships.

Once he turned professional, there was nothing holding Kareem back. He could dunk the ball as he pleased. However, he found that more than the vicious dunk, it was the graceful hook that was more potent. As he unleashed it on the NBA, there was nothing that anybody could do to stop it, as the ball seemed to swoop down from the sky. Eddie Doucette, the radio announcer in Milwaukee, where Kareem first played, in a moment of epiphany, immortalized it as the "skyhook".[14]

Kareem went on to have, arguably, the greatest career that a basketball player has ever had. He won the MVP of the league 6 times, MVP of the finals 2 times, and was chosen an all- star for 19 years. He retired as the all-time scoring leader in the NBA, after having scored 38,367 points, many of which with his cherished skyhook shot.[15]

Suggested Internet search:
Kareem Abdul-Jabbar Skyhook interview

GOING BANANAS

*The human race has only one really
effective weapon and that is laughter.*

— Mark Twain

Dani Alves had been facing racial taunts ever since he moved to Europe from his native Brazil. The fact that he was one of the best right backs in football (soccer) had never seemed to make any difference. It is one thing when the opposing fans boo you; as a competitor, you don't mind the passion of the fans. However, when those fans insult you for being dark-skinned, it becomes personal.

The football federations have attempted, in vain, to eliminate this ugly stain on what is considered, by many, to be the most beautiful game in the world. Clubs are fined, fans are expelled from matches; and yet, this despicable behavior, by a small but vocal minority of fans, continues. Fed up with the spectators' taunts and jeers, Dani Alves had called fighting racism a "lost war".[1]

In April 2014, Alves was playing for the famous Spanish football club, Barcelona, against Villarreal. Throughout the game, some of the Villarreal fans were taunting Dani Alves with monkey chants. Dani was used to these by now, and he continued to play with his usual panache.

The Barças were down. The score was 2-0 in favor of Villarreal.[2] The game was into the second half. Dani was about to take a corner kick. Suddenly, an object from the stands landed just in front of him.[3] It was a banana—an insulting act with which Dani Alves was all too familiar.

Over the years, Dani had seen it all; crowds had taunted him, calling him an ape. They had mocked him with loud monkey hoots. And they had thrown bananas at him. These were classless acts, done in cheap taste, and prompted by vulgar sentiments. Such occurrences were prevalent throughout Europe, notably in Spain, though he had been playing football there for the past several years. This banana before him was more of the same: prejudice and disrespect.

Dani did not have much time to think. He could, of course, have lost his temper. But to a professional football player, playing the game is their job and the football pitch their work spot. Getting angry would cause them to lose focus and prevent them from performing effectively and efficiently.

Dani could have done as those before him, and left the field. In 2011, Roberto Carlos, a renowned footballer from Brazil, walked off the field while playing in a Russian league match, when a banana was similarly thrown at him.[4] In January 2013, Kevin-Prince Boateng, a player from Ghana, who had been playing for the Italian Club of AC Milan, was targeted for racial abuse by fans of the opposing club. The same racial taunts got under his skin. Unable to stand it any longer, he kicked the ball into the crowd, ripped off his jersey, and led his team off the ground.[5] After the game, he tweeted with frustration, "Shame that these things still happen... #Stopracismforever."[6]

A walk-off, probably, would have been the best possible outcome for the Villarreal fans; they would have thought that *they* had intimidated an opposing player or team to flee the field. The spectators could have even felt empowered, that they could accomplish what their team could not: overwhelm an opponent with their tactics. A walk-off would have been conceding defeat to the Villarreal fans—only emboldening them to repeat their behavior, even more so aggressively in the future.

Daniel Alves was not going to allow himself to be perturbed, intimidated, or even distracted by such racist insults from pathetic fans. He was not going to give them the mental edge that they sought. He was a professional, and the fans were not going to deter him from doing his job, and doing it well.

Reminiscing about the incident later, he said, "We have suffered this in Spain for some time. We aren't going to change things easily. You have to take it with a dose of humor...If you don't give it importance, they do not achieve their objective."[7]

Without a moment's hesitation, Dani Alves bent down and picked up the banana. He peeled it. And he took a bite of it.

He then proceeded to take the corner kick, and coolly went about his business of playing the game. His club responded to his action, and rallied through the rest of the match. They continued to fight back on the pitch, and scored three goals to win 3-2.[8]

Afterwards, Dani Alves also posted the video of his act of eating the banana, on Instagram, with an accompanying message in Portuguese: "My father has always told me: son, eat bananas, which prevent cramps, how did you guess it? Haha."[9]

In this battle against racism, Dani put his humor and presence of mind to great and effective use, and appropriately shamed the abusers. He conveyed a declarative message: We will not allow you to beat us emotionally. We are not afraid of you. We will not run away from you. We think that your actions are silly.

It was a small act by a man, but a giant gesture against racism.

The response to Dani's action was immediate and positive. Several football players from around the globe posted pictures of themselves with a banana, to express their solidarity with him. Mario Balotelli, an Italian striker of African origin, who himself had been subject to racist taunting, posed with a peeled banana.[10] Several fans posted pictures of themselves with the same fruit. A simple act had snowballed into an avalanche of social awareness and support. The movement even gained enough momentum and prominence, for the Italian Prime Minister, Matteo Renzi, to join in. He posed for a photograph with a banana, standing alongside the coach of the Italian national football team.[11]

With a simple act, Dani Alves had communicated a very powerful message. Later on, he explained to Radio Globo, "I think that a negative reaction has to be met with a positive one. That makes more difference than fighting in a different way. I am glad to have created this effect and hope it serves in some way to put a stop to these types of attitudes."[12]

Embracing the movement, Dani's teammate and Brazilian superstar, Neymar, posted a picture on Instagram. It was of him and his son, smiling and holding a giant stuffed banana.[13] The caption: #SomosTodosMacacos. #WeAreAllMonkeys.

Suggested Internet search:
Dani Alves eats banana thrown by fan

BEND, BUT DON'T BREAK

.

*If you can meet with Triumph and Disaster
And treat those two impostors just the
same...*

— Rudyard Kipling

Debbie Brill was seething with anger at herself. After all these years, her body was betraying her at the time when she needed it most—during the finals of the 1984 Los Angeles Olympics. Debbie, the veteran high jumper from Canada, was a favorite to win one of the medals. Unfortunately, just prior to the qualifying rounds, two days earlier, she had sprained her ankle during the warm-ups. Walking was a torture, let alone running and jumping. Part medications and part adrenaline had helped her grit and gut through the pain, and qualify for the finals, along with fourteen other jumpers.[1]

The bar was being raised steadily and, one-by-one, the jumpers were falling by the wayside. The competition was now down to just six jumpers from the group of fifteen. Three competitors had already cleared 1.97 meters—within Debbie's personal best of 1.99 meters, which she had cleared when she broke the world indoor high jumping record.[2] Debbie had failed in her first two attempts at this height. To have any chance of winning a medal, she had to succeed in this final attempt. She had done this before. Debbie told herself that all she had to do was ignore the pain and she would be able to do it again. For several glorious years, her body had dutifully responded to her demands, soaring to great heights. As Debbie completed her jump, the bar also came down alongside her, and landed with a thud. And just like that, her chance at an Olympic high jump medal also crashed with it.

This is part of what an athlete signs for. The three standing on the podium get the glory, but the rest return home with nothing to show for their years of dedication, determination, and self-denial. Sure, it was disappointing as hell—but Debbie was not going to let it crush her. She was going to fuel her anger in a positive direction, and still keep open the prospect of the "perfect jump" that would carry her to some new heights. It was a perspective that she had gained from years of competition—from experiencing the exhilaration of successes, and also the pain and despair of losses. She was going to be alright. But Debbie was not sure if another Olympian, who was having a brutal experience, would be.

Debbie was concerned about Zola Budd. Nobody, more so a teenager, deserved to go through, what Zola Budd had to in 1984. Up until a few months prior to the Olympics, Zola was a petite girl, running middle and long distance races, barefoot, in her native South Africa. The young, naïve teenager had been scalded by the death of her sister who had also been her best friend.[3] Running was the salve that she used to mollify her pain. This girl from Bloemfontein, South Africa, however, could run like a gazelle. She had run the 5000 meters in a World Record time. The record was not ratified officially, as this was during the apartheid era and South Africa was excluded from international sporting events.[4]

Zola could run fast, but in 1984, events in her life were changing at such lightning speed, that the World Record holder could hardly keep pace with them. South Africa had always been a magnet for gold-diggers; here was a gold mine waiting to be unearthed. Cash was exchanged with her father by a British tabloid, which then arranged for the entire family to be shipped to England. A legal loophole was discovered, and voila! Zola Budd was now a UK citizen, within a few months of arrival in England.[5] Track and field veterans, Sebastian Coe and Daley Thompson, were still in their prime, but the British media needed a brand-new track star, and they decided that Zola Budd would be it. The populace, which had but a passing interest in track and field compared to football and cricket, was glued to the TV sets as her races were telecast nationwide. Frenzied crowds, mobs of reporters, and platoons of cameramen chased this simple, rural girl wherever she went.

There was something more. Along with the cheering crowds came the protesters who made Zola into a symbol of South African apartheid. "Release Mandela!" the crowds chanted when she ran. She had to ask her coach, "Who is Nelson Mandela?"[6] That was not somebody she had learned about in school.

Zola's running was as good as had been advertised. In spite of the overwhelming distractions, she was able to set a World Record for the 2000 meter in July 1984.[7] With the UK citizenship suspiciously arriving on time,[8] Zola was made part of the British Olympic contingent to travel to Los Angeles, USA.

The women's 3000-meter race was built up as the marquee showdown of the 1984 Olympics. The American favorite was Mary Decker, the most decorated middle distance runner of her time, who had just about owned most of the records in her stellar career. The only jewel missing: an Olympic Gold.

While there was a pack of elite runners capable of winning gold, the media simplified it into Zola vs. Mary. The rural girl from South Africa, running barefoot, vs. the golden girl from California. The novice vs. the veteran. The evil face of apartheid vs. the arrogant American. Labeling was too easy. Why bother about the truth, when you could sell copies or generate TV ratings? Even casual fans, throughout the world, had taken sides. They were either for Zola or for Mary

The LA Coliseum was packed. The runners were walking around, trying to vent their nervous energy. Soon, the starting gun fired and the runners were off. A middle distance race, unlike a sprint, has an element of strategy. There are the front-runners, whose plan is to outrun the pack. There are those who trail and try to time their final burst; and there are those who stay in the middle of the pack and elbow their way forward, as the race progresses. To the spectators, all that is evident is a bunch of runners, jostling and jogging. Mary Decker decided to lead from the front and tire out the rest of the pack.

Then, the unexpected happened. Zola Budd, running barefoot as always, decided to go into the lead. She went around the pack and cut in front of Mary. Mary Decker's shoes spiked Zola's bare heel. Zola felt the pain but continued running. Mary's spikes again brushed Zola, after which Mary stumbled and crashed on the track.

Hollywood, nearby, could not have scripted a more dramatic scene. It seemed to be happening in slow motion. As Mary fell, she grabbed Zola's jersey, ripping the number 151 from her back. She rolled off the track on to the infield, and lay there sobbing, her Olympic dreams shattered. Zola and the rest of the runners continued.

That is when Zola started hearing the jeers raining down on her from the stands.[9] The crowd had decided that Zola had deliberately tripped Mary and was pouring its vitriol on her. Little did it matter that Zola was running in front, and Mary had tripped from behind. Zola was the villain who had brought down their star by foul means. They booed the teenager mercilessly.

Zola wanted to stop running; but to a runner, quitting in the middle of a race is tantamount to sacrilege. She dreaded the thought of standing on the podium and facing the crowd if she were to win a medal. She slowed down, and ended up finishing seventh, with a time of 8 minutes and 48 seconds, eleven seconds slower than her personal best.[10]

The worst was yet to come. Zola went back to Mary to find out how she was. She was feeling terrible for Mary, her childhood hero, whose picture had adorned her bedroom wall. The frustration and disappointment of Mary erupted as anger and bitterness towards Zola. As Zola tried to say, "I am sorry," Mary retorted, "Don't bother." Mary went on to blame Zola for her fall, even hinting that it was deliberate.[11]

"Zola tripped me. She cut in front of me...I do hold Zola Budd responsible for what happened."[12]

The media joined Mary in pointing fingers. Zola was disqualified from the race for impeding Mary. Better sense prevailed, however, as the track officials later reviewed the tape, and cleared Zola of any fault; her seventh position finish was restored.[13]

Zola's Olympic dream had veritably turned into a nightmare. Her support system was in shambles. Her trusted confidante, her sister, was dead. Her parents were separating. Her father was already left behind in UK due to a fallout with the rest of the family.[14] Here was an eighteen-year-old who had lived a sheltered life until earlier that year, exposed, exploited, and excoriated on the world stage. Debbie Brill felt that she had to do something for this girl. Her life experiences had given her a perspective that she wanted to share with Zola.[15]

Debbie Brill's stardom had started when she was a teenager, growing up near Vancouver, Canada. She was the second ranked high jumper in Canada, even at fifteen years of age. Debbie had a unique jumping technique. While everybody jumped facing the bar (with the straddle or the western roll techniques), Debbie Brill had discovered a new way to jump. She would jump backwards. They called it the Brill Bend in Canada. Dick Fosbury independently developed the same technique, nicknamed the "Fosbury flop"; he dramatically displayed it on the world stage at the 1968 Mexico Olympics, where he won the gold medal.[16]

As a shy fifteen-year-old, Debbie went to Sweden, with the Canadian team, for a track meet. The crowd was amused to see this gangly teenager trying to jump backwards in a goofy method. They were laughing and howling at her. Teenage life is hard enough with its painful self-consciousness. Standing in the middle of the stadium, being made into a spectacle, there was no place for Debbie to hide. She fought back her tears. All she could muster was a height of 4'11", well below her best of 5'6". Up until then, she had been told that she was a winner. Now, the crowd dismissed her as a clown.[17] Little did the world know then, that within the next 20 years, jumping backwards would become the norm, with almost all high jumpers using variations of the Brill Bend or Fosbury Flop.

Debbie's slender frame concealed a spirit that would not stay down for long. She continued jumping backwards using the Brill Bend technique and by 1976 was one of the best high jumpers in the world.

The Olympic games was coming to Montreal, Canada. Debbie was ranked fourth in the world and was a huge hopeful for the medal-starved Canadians.

The first task at hand for Debbie was to qualify for the finals. The bar was set at 5'8"- a height that she could jump even if she had just been woken up from her sleep. There was nervous energy all around—it was the Olympics. Debbie took the first leap. She slipped slightly on the wet tarmac. She could not clear the bar.

Debbie was not worried; this was just a slip due to the wet conditions. She changed her shoe and proceeded to make her next attempt.

For her second jump, she moved her starting mark two steps forward. She felt that she had made the height; but, yet again, the bar came crashing down. Debbie was amazed. The problem this time was that she had started the jump too late and had bumped the bar on her way up.

Debbie had one last attempt. She was completely out of sync. She still felt confident. She told herself,

"For God's sake, just do it. Don't be silly." She brushed the bar on the way up and brought it down with her for good measure on her way down. She was out of the Montreal Olympics and out in the worst possible way. She had "no-heighted". She had not cleared a single jump.[20]

It was absurd! It was ridiculous that she could have worked so hard and yet meet with such a futility. She was crushed and disappointed inside. But she could also see the silliness of what had happened. She laughed. It was a bad day and that was all. There was nothing that she could do about it.

Canada was devastated. Debbie had let everybody down. An entire nation had pinned its hopes for self-assurance on a tall girl leaping over a bar. The least that the public demanded now was for Debbie to mirror their frustration. Her laughing shocked a lot of people; some were even personally offended. She became the target for their anger for her seeming nonchalance, more so than for her failure. On Canadian Broadcasting Corporation Radio, commentator Bob Picken called Brill's reaction an unworthy moment. "Perhaps, even if you have to fake it, you should have shed a few tears."[21] She was labeled Debbie Brill, the choker. She was not a winner.

Labels or not, Debbie was going to keep jumping. She enjoyed the thrill of soaring high and the adrenaline rush of the competitions. She lived her life according to her rules and kept improving. She won the gold medal in the Commonwealth Games in 1978 and the World Cup in 1979, and was ranked the world's number one high jumper. She was rounding into peak form, in time for the Moscow Olympics. Her chance at an Olympic medal was scuttled again in 1980 due to the decision of Canada to join the US led boycott of the Moscow Olympics.[22]

Two years later, in Edmonton, came the moment—a moment where the talent, the practice, the preparations, and the competitive spirit, all come together to produce an effort which overawes the very athlete herself. It is for such moments that athletes live: Bob Beamon, when he demolished the long jump record in Mexico and went into a state of emotional ecstasy that he could not even stand up; Michael Jordan, against Portland, when he famously shrugged his shoulder, seemingly unable to explain his otherworldly shooting, after firing his umpteenth three-pointer.

As Debbie went into her jump, she lost all awareness of what height she was attempting. She had a certain feeling, a drive, an out-of-body experience. She let go and jumped. No, she *flew* over the bar. The bar had been set at 1.99 meters- a new world record. It was her greatest accomplishment, and it had come when nobody had expected it. Debbie was now the mother of a four month-old, baby boy. Ever the maverick, she had taken a break for her pregnancy in the middle of her promising athletic career, and had come back with her determination undiminished. The sports pages wanted to rename the "choker". She was now the "Bionic Mom!" Debbie was not going to let this carry her away. She went back to little Neal, her four-month old, who still needed to be fed, burped, changed and put to bed.[23]

Coming back to LA, in 1984, Debbie's untimely ankle injury had conspired to kill her hopes of an Olympic medal. Instead of feeling sorry for herself, Debbie was acutely aware of the mental anguish that young Zola Budd was going through. Debbie decided to support Zola at the lowest moment of the young girl's career. Debbie Brill, along with her friend, Katie Schmidt, an accomplished javelin thrower, wrote an open letter to Zola Budd that was published in the Los Angeles Times.

The letter stated, "...Few can imagine the emotional pain one suffers from the denial of our passions at such a level...such as the one you suffered in Los Angeles...Our concern is that so much has happened to you at such a young age that it is difficult to sort it all out...Your talent is obvious. You have so many years ahead to train and to compete, and it may not seem so now, but the rewards are infinite...we can only urge you to transcend the peculiarities of this last year, and go on to learn, grow and benefit from all that sport has to offer—a very clear and measurable approach to life."[24]

Suggested Internet search:
Mary Decker Zola Budd race 1984
Debbie Brill 1976 Olympics interview

OH SAY,
CAN YOU SEE

A timely benefit, — though thing of little
worth
The gift itself, — in excellence transcends
the earth

> — Thiruvalluvar
> (Translated by G.U. Pope)

"Ministers have written that [he] demonstrated the embodiment of the Good Samaritan, and spoke of him in their sermons. Coaches expressed sentiments that it was the kind of message in sports they hope to convey...Many have asked for tapes of the incident. Parents and teachers felt compelled to write."[1]

Rose Garden, Portland, Oregon, April 25, 2003. Game 3 of the first round of the NBA playoffs, between the Dallas Mavericks and Portland Trailblazers, was about to begin. Dallas had won the first two games at home. Portland was desperate.[2]

The players had come out earlier and had warmed up. They had stretched, and gone through their shooting drills. They were nervous, for, elimination from the playoffs was a near certainty with a loss; no team had ever come back from a 3-0 deficit to win a best-of-seven series in the NBA.[3] For the coaches, a defeat could mean not only disappointment, but also the prospect of job losses. Their future and livelihoods depended on the bouncing of an orange ball. They had gone through all the last-minute details and were hoping that their game plans would work.

A hush descended on the stadium; it was time for the singing of the national anthem. The coaches stood in front of the bench. The players were standing in midcourt, some swaying gently, others chewing gum as they tried to keep their nervous energy in check. The crowd was tense, but eager to cheer their team and boost their morale. They took their hats off and stood, with their right hands over their hearts.

The stadium announcer's voice came through the speakers, "And now, to honor America, and salute the men and women serving our country with our national anthem, please welcome, as voted by you the fans, our winner of the Toyota Get-the-Feeling-of-a-Star promotion, Natalie Gilbert."[4]

As her name was announced, 13 year-old Natalie, wearing a beautiful, black-and-white gown, and a sparkling necklace, stepped on the court. She took the microphone in her hand and managed a nervous smile.[5] She had practiced hard for this moment, but singing in front of 20,000 fans and so many TV cameras is something that is hard to simulate. Adding to her discomfort was the fact that she was not feeling well that day.[6]

There was a mild applause after which the entire stadium went silent. Natalie started to sing.

"Oh say, can you see
By the dawn's early light,
What so proudly we hailed
At the...stars' light...star light..."

Natalie froze. She had missed the lines and her mind just went blank.

Young Natalie shook her head. She clutched the microphone tightly with both of her hands. It was humiliating. She wanted to be anywhere but where she was: in front of this huge crowd, with live TV cameras broadcasting her moment of shame.

There was no place to go, nowhere to hide. Her hand went up to her face instinctively. She lowered the microphone from her mouth. A scattering of jeers from the crowd broke the silence in the stadium.[7]

Natalie turned around searching for support, a friendly face. There was nobody there that she knew. Disaster was unfolding; it seemed that this rendition of the anthem would be left half-sung, with only utter embarrassment to be remembered about it.

Suddenly, a tall, graceful man walked towards her. He put her arms around her and said, "Come on, come on...*starlight's last gleaming.*" He didn't bother to correct her initial mistake with the lyrics. He supported her microphone hand and brought it back up to her face.[8]

Natalie gathered herself and took a deep breath. She resumed singing. The fog of nervousness and fear had still not cleared from Natalie's mind.

"*Whose broad stripes and bright stars...*
Through the peri...lous fight..."

Natalie stumbled ever so slightly. This time, however, she had somebody holding her in support. With a calming hand on her shoulder, he was going to guide her through the minefield of a prospective nervous breakdown. It was clear that this man was no singer, as his deep-voiced singing was absolutely pitch-imperfect. Yet, his only concern was to help little Natalie get through this moment. He led her through the notes, giving her a much-needed assist on the basketball court.

Natalie was now back in her stride. She did not have to struggle to remember the words. She was singing confidently as she hit the high notes.

"*And the rockets red glare!*
The bombs bursting in air!"

AV effects of rockets and bombs played throughout the stadium, breaking Natalie's concentration. But the man beside her kept the pace, continuing to sing with her. Slowly, the players and coaches joined this duo. Even the crowd started to sing for the finale.[9]

"O'er the land of the free!
And the home of the brave!"

The anthem was completed gloriously.

Natalie felt a huge wave of relief. She had been saved from a lifetime of humiliation and shame. As she was walking off afterward, her savior said to her, "Don't worry, kid. Everyone has a bad game once in awhile."[10]

This potentially devastating incident ended up, on the contrary, making Natalie famous. From then on, she was asked to perform the national anthem often, even making appearances on CNN, Good Morning America, and The Tonight Show with Jay Leno.[11] None of it would have been possible without the spontaneous action of the man who helped her complete her rendition of the anthem in Portland.

That man was the then head-coach of the Portland Trail Blazers basketball team, Maurice Cheeks. In spite of the anxiety of his team facing a must-win game, Maurice Cheeks, known to many as Mo Cheeks, was sensitive to the needs of a little girl in distress, and had immediately jumped in.

Throughout his career, Mo Cheeks was known as a classy player, a fierce competitor, and a true leader. He had had a distinguished basketball career as a player with the Philadelphia 76ers, prior to becoming the coach of the Portland Trail Blazers. He had been a 4-

time All-Star and a member of the NBA all-defensive team in multiple seasons. He had also won an NBA championship with the 76ers.[12]

On that day, not only Natalie, but nearly everyone in the auditorium, had frozen. Nobody else had come to Natalie's side to help her. It was at that moment that Mo Cheeks stepped in. Afterwards, when recounting the event, he said, "I did not think about doing it before I did it. I just saw a little girl in trouble and I went to help her. I'm a father. I have two kids myself. I'd have wanted someone to help them if they could."[13]

Watching the game was Billy Cunningham, ex-coach of Maurice Cheeks from his 76ers days. Cunningham was proud of his ex-player: "What Maurice did brought tears to my eyes...But that was typical Maurice, to spontaneously do the right thing at the right time and generally without any fanfare."[14]

Suggested Internet search:
Mo Cheeks national anthem

READY, SHOOT, AIM

When you have to shoot...shoot! Don't talk.

— Tuco (Eli Wallach)
The Good, the Bad and the Ugly

For the shooters in basketball, there is no time to pause, none to reflect on the magnitude of the situation, not even to take aim. Catch, shoot, forget if you miss, and get ready for the next shot.

Steve Kerr was one of the best shooters that the NBA had ever seen.[1] He had all the traits of a great—a quick release, a smooth jumper, and ice-cold blood. As of 2015, he still holds the record for 3-point shooting accuracy in NBA at 45.40%.[2]

But for a significant time, Steve had not been getting a chance to play. His team, the San Antonio Spurs, had not seemed to need him; he had been consigned to the end of the bench, watching the games as a spectator. The competitor inside of him chafed at the situation. Life had been glorious, just a few years earlier.

Steve Kerr had arrived in San Antonio after a successful stint in Chicago, playing alongside Michael Jordan arguably the best player of all time. In 1997, Game 6 of the NBA Finals was on the line. During the final timeout, Jordan predicted that Steve's defender, John Stockton, would leave Steve open, to go and double-team Jordan.[3] He cautioned Steve to be ready to shoot. Shooting the ball in that pressure cauldron takes a special kind of mental toughness apart from the actual shooting skill. If you make the basket, you are the hero; on the other hand, if you miss...you are the goat who cost your team the Championship. You have no place to hide. It takes a very select few to face up to that kind of a challenge.

Steve responded, "I'll be ready. I'll knock it down." He decided that if he got the ball, he was "going to let it fly." Just as Jordan had predicted, Stockton left Steve open to double-team Jordan, who immediately passed the ball to Steve. With no hesitation, Steve swished the ball for the game-winner, and the Bulls won their Championship.[4] That shot is considered one of the greatest in NBA history.

Steve Kerr was brought to San Antonio after 1997 for this specific skill set: accurate marksmanship with ice cool temperament. Within two years of his arrival, the Spurs won the NBA Championship. However, as the years went by, Steve found that his role on the Spurs was gradually diminishing. The Spurs now had a plethora of young shooters. Only five players could be on the floor at any time. Steve was rarely one of them.

During the 2000-01 season, Steve's frustration reached a boiling point. He wanted to protest his coach's decision of not letting him play more, but he could not enter a screaming match with his fiery coach, Gregg Popovich, to show his displeasure. The passive-aggressive door seemed open.

Steve decided to sit on the floor during the games rather than on the bench.[5] His unhappiness was evident to all the players, the officials, and the entire stadium. He was making a silent public statement.

Gregg Popovich, a man-manager par-excellence, understood the situation. He recognized that Steve's action was due to frustration stemming from his innate competitive spirit and not one of insubordination. After a couple of games, he pulled Steve aside and said, "Your body language is terrible...I know you're not playing, but you're a pro who's always handled yourself well, and now you're not. It doesn't look right, and I need you on the bench."[6]

Steve realized that his coach was absolutely right. He returned to the bench. He kept practicing, knowing full well that he might never get to play a single minute in a game. He wanted to be ready, if and when he would be called to contribute.

As an NBA professional, he was expected to practice every day, work on his skills and conditioning, watch game films, get treated for his injuries, discuss strategies, plan for the next opponent, arrive well before a game, warm up and be ready, even if it was unlikely that he would see anything more than garbage time on the floor. Steve handled himself as a professional, just as his coach had wanted him to.[7]

Fast-forward to Game 6 of the 2003 NBA Western Conference Finals in Dallas, as Steve's San Antonio Spurs took on the Mavericks. The Spurs were leading the 7-game series, 3-2.[8] A victory would take them to the NBA Finals. A loss would result in a winner-take-all game 7.

Game 6 was not going the way San Antonio had wanted. Towards the end of the 3rd quarter, they were trailing by 15 points.[9] The Dallas Mavericks were swarming the great Spurs player, Tim Duncan, with multiple defenders, and leaving his fellow players open, daring them to shoot. Manu Ginobili, Tony Parker, Steven Jackson—all good players—were shooting blanks. None of them could hit an open field goal that night.

Shooting a basketball is not physical, at least not completely. An iota of doubt is all it takes for a screwup. When a player is confident, the ball flies from their hands. Self-doubt is catastrophic. It leads to hesitation or, worse, abject fear. Players rush their shots. They start throwing bricks. They pass up open looks. The offense stalls.

The Spurs were in need of a hero to rescue them. Coach Popovich called on the nearly forgotten Steve Kerr to enter the game. As Popovich recalled later, "We had to find somebody to knock down a shot. It seemed logical to call Steve Kerr."[10]

The trouble was that Steve had hardly played in the playoffs until then; he had not taken even a single shot in the first five games of the series.[11] But now, all of a sudden, he had to enter the most crucial part of the game to rescue the team that had not trusted him until then.

Steve was prepared and primed for this very moment...and he was ready. He did not enter the court so much as he bounced onto it. This was his time. There was no fear.

Within a few seconds of Steve entering, the Spurs guard, Steven Jackson, passed him the ball.

"He is in the left corner. He launches it. How about Steve Kerr in his first attempt..."

Nothing but net.

As the ball went through, Steve felt that "...this could be my night."[12]

He got the ball a second time. He was open for a split-second as Michael Finley came flying in to try and block him.

"Steve fires for 3!! Steve has tied it at 71."

His coach recalled the moment; "It was like a flood all at once, totally unplanned."

The ball came to Steve a third time.

"Kerr with another 3. Yes!! Another 3 from Steve Kerr."

Who said you can't be a child twice? The Spurs' bench had transformed into an ecstatic, high school varsity team, jumping with unabridged joy.

Steve was not finished. Tim Duncan had the ball. Steve's defender left him open to double-team Duncan—a suicidal tactic.

"Right now Dallas doesn't want to double team because this man has been killing.... He gets it back. He is going again...Can they defend him? He has hit another 3 ball."

Steve had taken four 3-point shots and had made them all. The Spurs won the game handily, advancing to the NBA finals.

On the podium after the game, Steve stated, "This is one of the best nights of my career. There is always a chance to have a moment...just one moment. Tonight was one of those."[13]

Years later, Steve was called on to coach the Golden State Warriors. In his very first year, he forged his team into a formidable unit, and led them to win the 2015 NBA Championship. Steve had been ready again.

Suggested Internet search:
Steve Kerr 1996 Championship shot
Steve Kerr 2003 playoffs

THE (UN)SPOILED BRAT

Integrity is doing the right thing, even when no one is watching.

— C.S. Lewis

He took the tennis world like not a mere storm, but a violent tempest. He was a simmering volcano that would explode the minute he felt that a wrong call went against him. There was no diplomacy, nothing courteous about his methods, even at the most venerated of venues—the All England Championships at Wimbledon.

Wimbledon 1981 should have been McEnroe's crowning glory. He had reached the pinnacle of the game by defeating Bjorn Borg, the five-time defending champion. Long after the championships, it was his infamous outburst in the first round that stayed in the news.

McEnroe was playing against his fellow American, Tom Gullikson. The linesman called one of McEnroe's shots out. McEnroe thought that the ball was on the line. He went to the chair umpire, to protest. "Chalk came up all over."

In typical, polite, British fashion, the chair umpire, Mr. James Edwards, responded, "It is a bit of a stretch, Mr. McEnroe. That was a good call."

McEnroe gave up any attempt at politeness or decorum. "You can't be serious, man!" he started. Raising his pitch, and pausing with each word, he screamed, "YOU CANNOT BE SERIOUS!!! That ball was on the line!"

With hands going up for dramatic effect, "Chalk flew up! It was clearly in. How can you possibly call that out? Everyone knows it's in, in the whole stadium, and you call that out?!"

Getting no response from the umpire, he walked away, but not before taking a parting shot, calling him "the absolute pits of the world".

The umpire calmly responded, "I am awarding a point against you, Mr. McEnroe."[1]

McEnroe had behaved like a boorish schoolchild, and had been dealt with just like that, given a demerit for bad behavior.

McEnroe went on to win the match, and eventually the tournament. But, he was not celebrated as a champion. Instead, he was mocked as the "Superbrat" by British tabloids.[2]

Throughout his career, McEnroe kept up this pattern of behavior. He would throw his racket in anger, smash it on the ground, scream at umpires, and mock the linesmen, seemingly lowering the bar for norm and etiquette every time he played. He was fined multiple times, docked penalties, and was even disqualified from tournaments for his behavior. The writers delighted in outdoing each other calling him names: "petulant,"[3] "spoiled," "vain," "obnoxious," "crybaby."[4]

"I have got to say, it's an honor to meet you."[5] These were not words that McEnroe was used to hearing. Even more shocking to him was to hear this from President Nelson Mandela. From a sycophantic fan, perhaps, but to hear this from Mandela himself was something else.

President Mandela was an avid sports enthusiast. He had been a boxer in his earlier years. Even while incarcerated by the South African government for fighting against racial injustice, he had kept up with the world of sports through newspapers and the radio. One of Mandela's favorite memories was the 1980 Wimbledon finals, between Bjorn Borg, the unflappable Swede, and John McEnroe, the volatile upstart.[6]

Tennis fans, to this day, remember it as one of the greatest matches ever. Borg was going for his fifth, consecutive, Wimbledon crown, and the 20 year-old American, McEnroe, was trying to rip it from Borg's hands. The fourth set tiebreaker was mythical. Trailing the match, two sets to one, McEnroe was holding on for dear life. He had already fought off two match points. In the tiebreaker, he faced five more match points. One mistake and the game would have been over, and the championship lost. He served, he volleyed, he grunted, he dove, and he refused to lose. The tiebreaker went on for 34 points before McEnroe finally broke through to win the set 18-16. Alas, Borg, the champion, would not go down easily either. Borg won the final set, and his fifth consecutive Wimbledon championship.[7]

It was just a matter of time before McEnroe would take over the tennis world. He was a wizard on the court. The racket was his wand from which he conjured tennis shots that were pure magic. Not for him were the elaborate backswings or the violent forehands. He would caress the ball, coax and cajole it to seek impossible angles on the tennis court; the ball would willingly do his bidding. Tennis fans were treated to artistry on the court between 1980 and 1984 by this imperfect genius. They got their money's worth when they saw a McEnroe drop volley—the rest of the game was a bonus. In the monochromatic atmosphere at Wimbledon, this artist, with his brilliant red headband, had painted masterpieces using his wooden racket.

This was the same wooden racket that McEnroe handed to President Nelson Mandela when he met him several years later. McEnroe couldn't help but notice that Mandela was holding the racket "like he had played before" and "seemed happy to have it."[8]

Mandela maintained his regal bearing even at his advanced age. Twenty-seven years of imprisonment had not left a trace of bitterness in this legendary statesman, as he was attempting to lead a unified South Africa out of its darkness of the apartheid era. Compared to this magnanimity, McEnroe could see how trivial his grudges were towards linesmen and referees for blowing calls in a tennis match. He thought that Mandela was the most magical person that he had ever met; somebody who was "like an angel on earth."[9] That was when Mandela surprised him with his comment, that it was an honor for him to meet McEnroe.

A million dollars: that was the sum John McEnroe was offered to play an exhibition game against Borg, in Bophuthatswana,[10] considered "one of the phony 'independent' states set up by South Africa."[11] The year was 1981. McEnroe had just captured his first Wimbledon title. He was a hot commodity and everybody wanted a piece of him, including the South African government.

The apartheid government was trying to thumb their nose at the sporting boycott against South Africa. They would offer unprecedented amounts of money to athletes, to entice them to break the ban and tour South Africa.[12]

The international sports community, due to South Africa's racially abusive policies known as apartheid, had adopted the sporting ban. South Africa's non-white people were barred from participating in representative sport. Only whites could compete and be selected for the national teams.[13] Even as spectators, non-whites were subjected to rigid racial segregation: they had separate entrances, seating enclosures and toilet facilities, many of which were inferior to what the whites used. At some arenas, non-whites were banned altogether.[14]

This South African government was offering a million dollars to McEnroe to break the ban. A million dollars is a lot of money even today, but in 1981 it was an ungodly sum of money for a tennis player. To put it in perspective, McEnroe's prize money for winning at Wimbledon was a mere £21,600, or approximately $41,000.[15]

McEnroe had quite a few excuses to justify taking the money. For one, he was a professional, and, he had every right to earn his livelihood by playing tennis. Besides, several sportsmen and even entire countries had defended their involvement with South Africa, by stating that sports and politics should not mix. Several other tennis players were going to South Africa and taking the money. Jimmy Connors, well, he was no role- model. But even Chris Evert, the "Ice Maiden," who was a picture of perfection on the court, and Billie Jean King, who had a strong sense of social awareness, would go eventually.[16]

McEnroe however did not take the bait. He had a discussion with Arthur Ashe, the African-American tennis great, who had championed against apartheid South Africa.[17] McEnroe's logic was very simple: "Well, if they're offering me this obscene amount of money just to play one match, there must be something really wrong." He called the match off as he felt that "it was the right thing to do." In doing so, John McEnroe became the first, prominent, white athlete to reject the riches offered by South Africa.[18]

Several years later, McEnroe was thrilled on meeting President Mandela. He had been told by Mandela himself that it was an honor for him to have met McEnroe. That was one of the greatest things that anybody had said about him. This memory itself, he thought, "... was worth a million. No. Way more than that."[19]

Oh, if only he had a tape-recorder. Later, the Superbrat mused, "I just wish I could play this for all those *$@!&%^$ who said I was a jerk."[20]

Suggested Internet search:
John McEnroe you cannot be serious
McEnroe Borg Wimbledon 1980 tiebreaker

C'est La Vie

The most sublime act is to set another before you.

— William Blake

"Do they need help or not?" Larry Lemieux had to decide. If he were driving a car, it would have been easy. Turn around. Stop and ask. But, sailing in wind gusts of 35 knots with 12-foot waves crashing all around was a completely different matter.[1] He could see an overturned boat with one sailor nearby and another sailor a little farther. In an Olympic sailing race, where the difference of a fraction of a second could be crucial, Larry did not have the luxury of time, to deliberate and ponder.

Rule 1.1 of the International Sailing Federation states that "A boat or competitor shall give all possible help to any person or vessel in danger."[2] The question was whether these sailors were really in any danger. A capsized sailing boat, by itself, is not that uncommon a sight in a sailing race. It's only a matter of when, not if, a dinghy (boat) will capsize. Righting a capsized boat is part of a sailor's training—like getting back on the road for a fallen cyclist...only a thousand times more difficult. So, did these sailors need Larry's help? Even if they needed help, couldn't the rescue boats handle the job? They would be here any moment. Should he try to go and find out? He could, but Larry would have to kiss his chances of medalling in the 1988 Olympics goodbye.

Lawrence Lemieux, one of the most accomplished Canadian sailors of his time, had his best chance at an Olympic medal this time. What had started years ago as a fun experience with his five brothers in Edmonton, Canada, had now grown in to a lifetime pursuit and an Olympic dream.[3] He had arrived in

Seoul as one of the top ranked sailors in the world in Finn class racing.

Larry loved the challenge of sailing solo in a Finn dinghy. "It's you and the boat," according to him. "You're in control of your destiny, you can develop a technique that works for you. It's all you."[4] The Finn is a wild mustang to the uninitiated. However, an experienced sailor can tame it into a Kentucky Derby thoroughbred. The Finn is a true test of tactical and technical sailing skills, and blesses its faithful with "developing strength of character, perseverance, tenacity and the challenge of doing something difficult really well."[5]

The sailing competition for the 1988 Olympics was held in Pusan, South Korea. There were eight classes of events, and for each event, seven races were scheduled. The top six results were tallied and used to determine the winner. Larry was getting mixed results in the races. He had finished 13th on day one, and 5th in his second race. The next two days were worse, as he had placed 20th and 12th.[6] He had to make his mark in the fifth race, failing which, his dream of a medal would very well stay only a dream. If he did well, on the other hand, the disappointing 20th place finish from day three could be eliminated from his final tally.

The start of a sailing race is fascinating in itself. Unlike in a car race, one cannot park the boat behind the starting line. Instead, the sailors set their watches to the exact time as to when the race would start. The boats, with their tall masts and sails, look like a grazing herd of languid brachiosauruses in Jurassic Park, wandering lazily, as the sailors slowly maneuver them to reach an advantageous position, close to the starting line without crossing it. This involves not only skill but also tact, and a great understanding of wind speed, direction, water current, and awareness of what the other boats are doing, among several other factors. Even recognizing the starting line, which has to be more so visualized than seen, takes considerable experience.[7]

The race was on, and off went the boats. They were picking up speed and were skimming the surface of the water like majestic dolphins. Unlike the large keel boats, used in races like the America's Cup, that plough through the water, these planing boats appear to almost leap out of the seas. The sailors were hiking out (stretching outside the boat for balance) to their limits, in order to properly maneuver the boats. The wind was spraying surf all over. It was a fantastic spectacle.[8]

Larry had a great start and was briefly in the lead, but fell back into second place after a short while—still a good position. As he turned to his right, the capsized boat caught his eye. It was a 470-class two-person boat, from another race that was occurring on this course simultaneously.[9]

One sailor appeared to be hanging on to the board for dear life while the other was a distance away. The second sailor appeared to be being pushed further from the boat by the waves. There was no rescue boat nearby.[10]

The sea was getting rough. Visibility was poor. The waves were cresting as high as twelve feet, he estimated. They were making it very hard to locate the orange course markers, which were only about eight feet tall.[11] Even if the rescue boat arrived, locating a bobbing head in the sea, Larry surmised, was going to be like searching for the proverbial needle in a haystack. He yelled out to the sailors to find out if they needed help. With roaring waves and gusting winds, he could not make out what the reply was. Larry had to decide now.[12]

He later recounted the event: "The first rule of sailing is, you see someone in trouble, you help him. My thought process was: do they really need help, because, a lot of times you are able to save yourself. But I couldn't understand if they were saying yes or no. I just had to go. If I went to them and they didn't really need help, *c'est la vie* (that's life). If I didn't go, it would be something you would regret for the rest of your life. But I wasn't thinking that at the time...At the time, you just go."[13]

Larry had decided to go to the aid of his fellow sailors. The boat belonged to the Singapore sailing team of Shaw Her Siew and Joseph Chan. Siew was pinned under the boat, having suffered a cut, and was bleeding. The boat's rudder was broken; it was virtually useless to sail. Chan was drifting steadily away from the boat. A rescue boat may have been able to reach Siew, but was extremely unlikely to spot Chan. He was at a very high risk of being swept by the current and lost at sea.[14]

The decision was made, but the task was not going to be easy. For one thing, the current was against the wind, and the waves were breaking. It was like a one-story building of water crashing onto Larry's boat. He also had to forego the usual "man-overboard" rescue technique, of sailing upwind. He had to sail downwind, against the current, to get to Chan. Sailing downwind meant that he could not slow down as he approached Chan; instead, he sailed next to him and used his strength to flip him on to the boat.[15]

Larry then headed back to help Siew. The Finn is too small a boat to get three people on board. Larry, therefore, had to hold his boat upright and steady, and stay next to them for support, until the rescue boat arrived.[16]

The two capsized sailors were rescued, but Larry Lemieux had unfinished business. There was still an Olympic race to be completed. He returned to the race, but was only able to finish 21st out of a field of 32. The Olympics sailing committee did recognize the extenuating circumstances and restored his second position for the race. Larry, however, was not able to improve upon his performance, and did not medal in the 1988 Olympics. Had the rescue efforts taken a toll on his physical and mental reserves? One can only speculate, for Larry did not offer an excuse.

In fact, Larry did not compete in any Olympics after 1988. Yet, he has no regrets, later stating, "What I did, anyone would've done. What had to be done. It was no different than seeing someone in a car by the side of the road who's obviously in distress, who might've had a heart attack, who obviously needs help...Doesn't happen very often that anyone is put in that position, but you stop. You help."[17]

However, Larry's act was considered extraordinary, even by Olympic standards. He had exemplified human spirit, the celebration of which the Olympic games are held. He was awarded the prestigious Pierre de Coubertin Medal, named in honor of the founder of the International Olympic Committee, and father of the modern Olympics. This award, considered to be one of the noblest honors that can be bestowed upon an Olympic athlete, is given to those who demonstrate the true spirit of sportsmanship. Only five people had previously been endowed with that medal, throughout the long history of Olympics. While bestowing the award, the President of the IOC, Mr. Juan Antonio Samaranch, declared, "By your sportsmanship, self-sacrifice and courage, you embody all that is right with the Olympic ideal."[18]

Suggested Internet search:
Lawrence Lemieux sailing

ATTENTION TO DETAILS

It has long been an axiom of mine that the little things are infinitely the most important.

— *Sherlock Holmes*
Sir Arthur Conan Doyle

It was the first day of the squad meeting. The UCLA basketball team had gathered in the gym. There were the wide-eyed freshmen, a blend of excitement and nerves, eager to show that they belonged. And the upperclassmen, who had their inside jokes and "been-there, done-that" looks.

And then there was Coach John Wooden—not an imposing figure, dwarfed by several of his players, with an appearance more befitting your friendly small-town bank manager than a collegiate basketball coach. He stood at 5'10", with a thinning hairline and a few black strands breaking the monotony of the silver, black-rimmed eye glasses, and a gentle smile, somehow holding court, commanding the attention and conveying the message silently: "No nonsense will be tolerated!"

UCLA basketball was simply the most dominant college basketball program that had ever been. The team had won 10 National Championships in a span of 12 years, with seven in a row. The team had once won 88 consecutive games.[1] The performance of the team in every game was like that of a symphony: prepared, practiced and pitch-perfect, guided by John Wooden's baton.

Wooden was a brilliant basketball coach, perhaps even the best ever. Under his direction, UCLA was always meticulously prepared, supremely conditioned, and fearless to compete at the highest level against any of their opponents.

Coach Wooden, however, considered himself a teacher, first and foremost. To his students, he was a mentor, a guide. He taught the students much more than basketball; he taught them how to learn.[2] As one of his favorite students, Bill Walton said, he gave "...the opportunity to train your mind, to learn how to think, to develop skills, to make decisions, to dream, to achieve peak performance."[3] According to Walton, "Coach Wooden never talked about winning and losing, but rather about the effort to win. He rarely talked about basketball, but generally about life. He never talked about strategy, statistics, or plays, but rather about people and character. Coach Wooden never tired of telling us that once you become a good person, then you have a chance of becoming a good basketball player."[4] The wizard of Westwood, as coach Wooden was referred to, was indeed the Albus Dumbledore of UCLA basketball.

John Wooden's definition of success was unique: "Success is mine when I work my hardest to become my best, and that I alone determine whether I do so."[5]

The first coaching session was not going to be anything about basketball. No lectures on strategies. No motivational speeches. Coach John Wooden was going to teach the students something that they had done daily, probably since the day they got out of diapers. It was going to be his famed lesson on "shoes and socks."[6]

"You know, basketball is a game that's played on a hardwood floor," Wooden said. "And to be good, you have to...change your direction, change your pace. That's hard on your feet. Your feet are very important. And if you don't have every wrinkle out of your sock..."[7]

It was a sight to behold: the wise old coach, with utmost earnestness, was teaching his college students the most trivial task of putting on their socks. The tall, strapping teenagers were all eyes and ears as the coach was going about his demonstration, with the same attention to details as a sniper would while cleaning his rifle.

"Roll the socks down over the toes, ball of the foot, arch and around the heel, then pull the sock up snug so there will be no wrinkles of any kind."[8]

It was the students' job, next, to demonstrate to the teacher that they had mastered the skill of wearing their socks! No half-measures. The coach's standards were exacting on the minutest of details. This was a craft, and the process had to be perfected. He wanted the whole exercise to be done "conscientiously, not quickly or casually..." with "absolutely no folds, wrinkles or creases of any kind on the sock."[9] He was going to watch over them and make sure that they got it right.

The students then had to carefully go over the socks with their fingers, to ensure that there were no folds or creases.

"Now pull it up in the back, pull it up real good, real strong. Now run your hand around the little toe area...make sure there are no wrinkles and then pull it back up. Check the heel area. We don't want any sign of a wrinkle about it...The wrinkle will be sure to get you blisters, and those blisters are going to make you lose playing time..." [10]

The next task to be mastered was to lace up and tie a shoe. Shoes had to be a perfect fit. On arrival, it was the custom in most institutions to ask the students for their shoe size, and get them their shoes. But Coach Wooden was not going to leave that to chance. Each student had been measured on arrival at UCLA, to find his perfect shoe size.[11]

The lace had to be inserted snugly, putting some pressure on each eyelet as it went through. Once the shoe was worn, the lace had to be double-knotted on each shoe, ensuring a tight fit.[12]

This exercise was not simply a ritual. Coach Wooden believed in the basics: attention to, and perfection of tiny details that might commonly be overlooked. They may have seemed trivial, even laughable, to an outsider. But he felt, "Shoes that are a little too big let the foot slide around. This can cause a blister..." A blister in the foot would prevent the athlete from performing at his best. Likewise, an untied shoe could come off during a game. This would adversely affect a player's performance. According to Wooden, if there was a method to maximize the chance of success and reduce the likelihood of failure, it was the responsibility of the coach and the player to follow it.[13]

The students had been given the first lesson on the fundamentals to progress in basketball, business and life. They had been taught the "difference between champions and near-champions."[14]

THE LOVABLE
BADASS

And how shall you punish those whose remorse is already greater than their misdeeds?

— Kahlil Gibran

He was combustible. He was tenacious. He was skilled. He was emotional. He was scary. He was a fierce competitor who took no prisoners when he played. He was as likely to grab a rebound in traffic, literally tearing it away from his opponents, as to send a vicious forearm across the face of an unsuspecting opponent. As likely to stop his dribble and pop a three pointer, as to get a technical foul for doing something stupid or vengeful on the court. He played with an edge, an angry scowl, and was a bulldog on defense. He was Ron Artest.

Ron Artest could play basketball. There was no denying his talent and passion for the game. He had won the NBA Defensive Player of the Year in 2003-04 and had been selected four times to the NBA All-Defensive team.

Ron Artest was also a ticking time bomb, with an unpredictable timer, just waiting to erupt with a violent act on the basketball floor at any time. He was considered by many to be a "headcase."[2] Everyone knew that there were only two things in the world you didn't mess with: Texas and Ron Artest.

Ron gained national notoriety on November 19, 2004. He was playing for a talented Indiana Pacers team against the Detroit Pistons. The game was at the home stadium of the Detroit Pistons—the Palace of Auburn Hills, Michigan—and was nationally televised on ESPN.[3]

The teams despised each other. The previous year, Detroit had defeated Indiana in the playoffs.[4] The Pacers were trying to prove that this year was going to be different. Ron played brilliantly, and his team was up by 15 points with less than a minute to go in the game. The game had been chippy, with the fouls getting harder by the minute.[5] Tension was building. Something...something was about to happen.

As Detroit's Ben Wallace was about to score, Ron Artest fouled him hard; he clobbered him. It was not technically an illegal play, but needless in the context of a game that was just about decided. Ben Wallace took exception to it and shoved Ron Artest against the basket support. And all hell broke loose.[6]

Players were shoving each other. Ben Wallace was agitated and people were trying to hold him back. Ron tried to calm himself. He had been told earlier: "If you see yourself getting too excited, disengage and get yourself out of it and get your thoughts together."[7] He put on a set of headphones, and went and laid down on the scorer's table. Just then, a fan threw a beverage that landed on his face.[8]

That was it. Ron Artest came undone. He ran into the stands like an enraged bull. A coach tried to get in the way to stop him. Ron ran over him like an eighteen-wheeler over a Prius. He pushed a fan down and shook him vehemently, asking if he had thrown the beverage. Other fans were joining the melee. Stephen Jackson, Ron's teammate, joined him in the stands.[9]

Punches and chairs were thrown. It was complete mayhem. Nobody had ever seen the likeness of this in North American Sports.[10]

Ron Artest was suspended a total of 86 games for this fight. He lost close to five million dollars because of his suspension.[11] The image of an angry, violent, out-of-control Artest was etched in the mind of every fan.

This was the same Ron Artest who in later years hobnobbed with Presidents Barack Obama and Bill Clinton,[12] who was given the ceremonial keys to Las Vegas on "Ron Artest Day" held in his honor,[13] and who was awarded the 2010-11 Walter J. Kennedy Citizenship Award, given by the Professional Basketball Writers Association, for outstanding service and dedication to the community.[14]

Game 7 of the 2010 NBA finals. Winner gets to be the champion. Loser is forgotten in history. The superstar of the Los Angeles Lakers, Kobe Bryant, was struggling. His teammate, Ron Artest, was playing his heart out. He had been guarding Paul Pierce, the best player of the Boston Celtics, hounding him to a poor shooting night. With just over a minute to go and the Lakers barely clinging to a 3-point lead, Kobe passed the ball to Artest on the right wing. With no hesitation, Artest let fly a jumper that swished through the net. Ballgame. Championship.[15]

Later on, his coach Phil Jackson would say, "Ron Artest was the most valuable player tonight. He brought life to our team."[16] Ron Artest had won the coveted NBA Championship ring, the dream of almost every child who dribbles a basketball. He had also answered the question that had dogged him throughout his career: "Could [Ron] harness his impressive skills and temper and help his team without self-destructing?"

Immediately after he won the NBA championship, as he was interviewed, Ron said something on National TV that is not commonly heard.

"I'd like to thank my psychiatrist, Dr. Santhi. She really helped me relax...Thank you so much. So difficult to play, so much emotion going on in the playoffs, and she helped me relax."[17] On the biggest day of his professional career, he was not afraid to expose his mental illness to the entire nation.

Ron Artest had always had a problem with temper, even dating back to his childhood. Multiple times, he had been asked to go through psychotherapy. He had tried. He had failed. He had tried again. He had failed again. He had even ended up getting arrested after one of his anger-related issues. His arrest became a huge turning point in his life. He took his psychotherapy seriously, and fought to control his temper in earnest.[18]

After winning the NBA championship, Ron Artest decided to auction off his Championship ring: the ring for which he had worked throughout his career; the ring coveted by all players and cherished by all the champions as the crown jewel of their careers. No, he was not bankrupt. He wanted to donate the proceeds to charity.

The ring was sold for more than $650,000. Ron donated the money to high-risk youth suffering mental illnesses.[19] He had earlier founded Xcel University to encourage kids to further their education, as well as to "advocate for Mental Health Awareness and quality Mental Health Services for all."[20]

Ron Artest continued to shed light on mental health issues, especially in children and adolescents. He went to schools and mental hospitals. He opened up about his personal life, talked about being counseled for anger issues, parenting issues, marriage issues.[21]

He emphasized to children, "When it comes to mental health issues, you don't have to be afraid."[22] He urged youngsters to seek professional counselors. He even testified before the US Congress on behalf of the Mental Health in Schools Act.[23]

As though to emphasize his transformation, Ron changed his name to Metta World Peace. His first name, Metta, is a traditional Buddhist word that means "strong wish for the welfare and happiness of others."[24] He was, however, given a perhaps more appropriate nickname by artists in Toronto, who had been inspired by his life: "Lovable Badass."[25]

Suggested Internet search:
Malice at the Palace
Ron Artest thanks psychiatrist

A GOALKEEPER IN MIDFIELD

Better is one's own duty, though devoid of merit, than the duty of another well discharged. Better is death in one's own duty; the duty of another is fraught with fear.

— Bhagavad Gita III: 35

El Loco: the madman.[1] There was nothing conventional about him. With René Higuita, you had to be ready for the unexpected. If you watched a football game played by the Colombian national team or the club team Atlético Nacional, during the 1980s, it was very likely that you talked about René Higuita after the game.

Goalkeepers in football hardly ever get to be the center of attention. In fact, most of the time they get to be noticed only when they fail: when a goal is scored against them. Once or twice a game, they might make a great save. Otherwise, they stand in one corner of the field, biding their time. The fans are happy if their team's goalkeeper is bored. It usually means that their team is winning.

René Higuita always wanted to be more than just a traditional goalkeeper. He had started his football career as a center forward, but had eventually found his niche as a goalkeeper.[2] Standing at 5'9", with long, curly hair and a magnetic smile, he commanded and reveled in attention.[3] He considered himself an entertainer, who brought smiles to the fans' faces.

And those fans loved René Higuita. They would go to the game hoping that they might see the famous "Scorpion kick," Higuita's signature, self-invented move. All goalkeepers, when a ball comes to them, either catch it, deflect it, or kick it to one of their teammates. Well, all except for "El Loco." He would dive forward, facedown, under the ball. He would then bring his feet up over his head while still flying in midair, and clear the ball forward—just like a scorpion would bring its tail back up over its head. High risk, hardly any reward; but the crowd would go ecstatic.[4]

Higuita was also part of some of the set-piece actions of the Colombian team, and would take free kicks and penalties. He was fairly successful, scoring 44 goals throughout his career, including eight international goals.[5]

Higuita, however, wanted more. He probably wanted to prove to himself and to the fans that he transcended the role of goalkeeper. When he had to clear a ball, he would not pass it, but instead, dribble it way past the penalty box. It was a high-wire act. The fans were on the edge of their seats as there was nobody home, standing guard. The opposition knew that all they had to do was to take the ball away from Higuita and they would have an open goal to shoot at. It was theater and René Higuita was certainly the diva on stage.

Perhaps, the most defining point of René Higuita's football career came during the FIFA World Cup in 1990. Colombia had barely qualified for the second round, after scraping through their first. They had to face Cameroon in the round of 16. Even though Cameroon had topped their group by beating fancied teams like Argentina and Romania, most fans thought that Colombia had gotten a break.[6]

The match was tied scoreless at the end of regulation. Cameroon had brought in their 38-year-old super substitute, Roger Milla, in the second half. He had already scored 2 goals in the tournament against Romania.[7]

As overtime started, Roger Milla added to his goal collection by scoring the first one of the game. Cameroon 1, Colombia 0. Colombia was down, but not out yet.[8]

A few minutes later, Higuita was standing well outside the penalty box, positioned more like a sweeper than a goalkeeper. The ball came to Higuita. He looked up and saw a green, Cameroon jersey close to him. The safest option was for Higuita to clear the ball by blasting it—forward or towards the sidelines, but out of danger. Safety first was not how René Higuita played football.

Higuita decided to dribble and pull the ball back, a move he had made countless times. This time, however, it was not meant to be. Milla, the wily veteran, stole the ball from Higuita and started racing towards the goal. Higuita could only see a green blur as Milla flashed past him. No goalkeeper is going to catch a striker on a footrace, even if it is a 38-year-old striker. Higuita made a desperate dive to stop him. Milla took 2 long dribbles and deftly guided the ball into the empty net. Cameroon 2, Colombia 0.[9]

Higuita stared straight ahead. He had no place to hide. It was a moment of utter humiliation. His mistake had cost Colombia dearly as they went on to lose the game 2-1 and were eliminated from the World Cup.[10] The team had to pay a huge price for the individual theatrics of their star.

If he had learned anything from this incident, it was not apparent. A few years later, René was playing for his club, Aucus, against El Nacional in Ecuador. René was showing off his dribbling skills again. He dodged past several players and reached midfield. That was when his luck ran out. Again. Erik de Jesus, the right back of El Nacional, tackled him and relieved him of the ball. Erik blasted the ball from the 50-yard line into an empty net.[11]

For the second time in his career, the wild-haired goalkeeper was publicly shamed, far from home, stranded in midfield.

Suggested Internet search:
René Higuita scorpion kick
René Higuita Milla 1990

You Can't Measure Courage

I have fought the good fight, I have finished the race, I have kept the faith.

— 2 Timothy 4:7

Derek Redmond could not wait for the race to start. It was the semifinal of the 400-meter race at the 1992 Barcelona Olympics. Derek was sure that he would qualify for the final and eventually win a medal. The only question was what color the medal would be: gold or silver. He had won his first two round heats, and had also run the fastest time in the first round.[1] He was confident that this would be his turn, finally, unlike in Seoul.

At the Seoul Olympics in 1988, Derek had faced major disappointment. He had injured his Achilles tendon, and had to pull out of the race just minutes before it began. Injuries continued to plague his career. Over the next four years, leading up to the Barcelona Olympics, he had undergone a total of eight surgeries. Yet, he did not give up on his dream of an Olympic medal.[2]

In spite of his injuries, Derek had accomplished a lot in his stellar athletic career. He had held the British record for the 400-meter sprint, and had won gold medals as part of the famed British 4 x 400-meter relay team at the World Championships, the Commonwealth Games, and the European Championships.[3] But to any athlete, the Olympic medal is the ultimate dream. That day in Barcelona was one more step towards his lifetime goal.

The night before the race, Derek strategized with his father and his coach. Until then, he had been cruising through the qualifying rounds in order to conserve himself. In this race, however, he was going to try harder to get a good lane position for the finals.[4]

It was a beautiful day in Barcelona. The semifinal heat was about to start. The eight runners lined up in their respective lanes. Derek was in lane 5. He felt good on the starting blocks. The gun went off and Derek was the fastest to react.[5] He had a great start.

Derek's usual strategy was to get around the first bend and turn on the burners for about 30 meters and accelerate. This time around, by the time he had gotten into his stride, he was already past the first turn. He decided to conserve his energy in case he needed it for the final push.[6]

Disaster struck just then. When he reached the 150-meter mark, Derek heard a pop. He continued for two or three more strides. He then felt an excruciating pain in his hamstring. It felt as though somebody had pierced the back of his thigh with a hot knife and was twisting it around. He had torn his hamstring. The pain was unbearable. He grabbed the back of his leg and collapsed on the track.[7]

The stadium went into a hush. Derek was on the ground writhing in pain. The other runners continued.

Derek thought to himself, "There is no way I am going to be stretchered out of these Olympics."[8] He got up and tried hobbling, in spite of the intense pain.[9] The competitor in him believed that he could still overtake four other runners and qualify for the finals. He thought that he was running; he was but a pitiful figure, limping horribly.

Derek looked up at the field. It was all over for him. Most of the runners had crossed the finish line.[10]

But Derek was not going to give up. He was going to finish the race—even if it was the last race that he ever ran. He did not want a DNF (Did Not Finish) against his name.[11] Slowly, but with a steely determination, Derek hopped painfully on one leg, trying to complete the run that he had started.

The spectators were stunned to see this act of courage. A few medical personnel came on the track to try and stop Derek, but he would have none of that.[12]

Among the thousands watching from the stands, was Derek's father, Jim. He had accompanied Derek to Barcelona, as he did for all major competitions. Seeing his son hobbling, Jim pushed his way through the crowds and came to the track. He wanted to prevent his son from further hurting himself, by running on a torn hamstring.[13]

He came to his son's side, put an arm around him, and said, "Derek, it's me. You don't have to do this."[14]

"Dad, I want to finish," Derek replied. "Get me back in the semifinal."[15]

"OK. We started this thing together and now we'll finish it together." Jim helped Derek lean on him and they started walking towards the finish line.[16]

What was happening was completely unexpected and unprecedented. A parade of officials tried to intervene; they tried to prevent Jim and Derek from continuing.[17] Well, there are no rules or regulations against a father-son duo finishing a race. How do you even time the run?

"Force is measured in pounds. Speed is measured in seconds. Courage? You can't measure Courage."[18]

Nobody was going to stop the Redmonds. Jim pushed the officials away. His son wanted to finish the race and this father was going to do everything he could to help him. The officials could see the determination in their eyes, and backed off.

Derek, with tears in his eyes, was leaning on his father, and hobbled along. His father kept repeating to him, "You're a champion, you've got nothing to prove."[19] Father and son crossed the finish line together.

The entire stadium erupted in thunderous applause, watching this spontaneous act of courage and love. The British team captain, Linford Christie, embraced Derek as he finished the race. They both broke down in tears.[20]

Derek did not win the race. In fact, since he was helped across the finish line, he ended up receiving a DNF.[21] However, this moment remains an inspiration for thousands.

A Canadian athlete, whom Derek had never met, left this message for him at the Olympics, "Long after the names of the medalists have faded from our minds, you will be remembered for having finished, for having tried so hard, for having a father to demonstrate the strength of his love for his son. I thank you, and I will always remember your race and I will always remember you—the purest, most courageous example of grit and determination I have seen."[22]

Suggested Internet search:
Derek Redmond Olympics 1992

THE REAR ADMIRAL

A leader...is like a shepherd. He stays behind the flock, letting the most nimble go out ahead, whereupon the others follow, not realizing that all along they are being directed from behind.

— Nelson Mandela

For David Robinson, nothing had ever been difficult on the basketball court. But this...this was hard. Ever since his arrival in San Antonio to play for the Spurs, David had been the unquestioned leader of the team. However, now his position did not seem as pre-eminent as it had been.

David Robinson had rescued the San Antonio Spurs from the depths of irrelevance. The season before he arrived, the team had lost 61 of its 82 games.[1] When David made his appearance, the team, even the entire league, had not seen a player who played the center position like him. He was a Lamborghini on the court—a spectacular sight to behold. 7'1" in height with a chiseled physique,[2] David had an otherworldly ability to jump, a soft shooting touch, and quickness that belied his frame. He could score, rebound, block shots, pass, and pretty much do anything and everything as good or better than any of the other players on the team, if not in the entire league. It was as though, nature had, in a moment of inspiration, created a prototype for the perfect basketball player.

David took the league by storm as he turned the Spurs' fortunes completely around with his all-around game. The Spurs won 56 games in his first year, a dramatic improvement from the previous.[3] He easily secured the title, Rookie of the Year.[4]

David continued to blaze a glorious trail over the next several years, leading the league in rebounding in 1990-91 and 1995-96, blocks in 1990-91 and 1991-92, and in points scored in 1993-94. He scored 71 points in the last game of that season to win the scoring title. He was awarded the Defensive Player of the Year in 1991-92 and Most Valuable Player of the league in 1994-95. The Spurs were now consistently among the best teams in the league and they owed it to David Robinson. He was fondly referred to as "The Admiral" in acknowledgement of both his leadership skills and the fact that he graduated from the United States Naval Academy prior to joining the Spurs.[5]

But everything changed in 1996. David Robinson suffered a back injury, and played only 6 games that season. The Spurs' record nose-dived in his absence, as they won an abysmal 20 games. Because of their terrible finish, the Spurs had an opportunity to get a good player in the NBA draft. As luck would have it, the Spurs acquired the first pick in the draft.[6]

Tim Duncan, the 6'11" senior from Wake Forest, was considered almost universally as the best player in the draft that year.[7] The Spurs selected him first overall. Here was a younger version of David who played nearly the same position (Tim liked to be referred to as a power forward and not as a center), and could do several of the things that David did just as well, if not better.

As the year went by, David found that the ball was going more to Tim Duncan and less so to himself. Tim was getting more opportunities to score while David's shot attempts were down. David was now becoming the second most important player of the team instead of its unofficial king.

David Robinson had never experienced such a situation in his professional career. He was always "the man" of the team. When a basket was needed, he was the one that the team depended upon. The ball had always come to him. This situation should have grated on his professional pride.

Many a team had been torn apart from internal conflicts between two superstars. Teams had to end up being dismantled because of personality and ego conflicts. In fact, just a few years later, the LA Lakers would end up being broken up due to the inability of its two superstars, Shaquille O'Neal and Kobe Bryant, to coexist.

The common paradigm in sports was that a team was like a wolf pack in which there was no space for two alpha males. But, David Robinson was basketball royalty; he was trying to establish a dynasty rather than a foraging group of mongrels. He had to train the Crown Prince to take over the reins.

He welcomed Tim Duncan and began to mentor him. He invited Tim to his home, and showed him what it is to be a professional in the league. He taught him the mental aspects of the game, which he had learned through his years of experience. He gracefully accepted his new, secondary role in the team. Allowing Tim to get the accolades as the main scorer, David took on what is generally referred to as the "dirty work"—rebounding and playing defense. He rebounded and blocked shots with the same enthusiasm and ferocity as before, while taking fewer shots and opening up opportunities for Duncan.[8]

With the two big men patrolling the middle, the Spurs were an unstoppable force in 1999, and they won their first-ever NBA Championship.[9] David had accomplished what he had to set out to achieve when he had joined the team—to bring a championship to his beloved city and its beleaguered fans.

In fact, David gave back even more to the city. He and his wife donated several million dollars to build a school for underprivileged children in San Antonio.[10] David Robinson was not only a foundation of the team, but also a pillar of the community.

The legacy of David's magnanimity and commitment to the team's cause still endures in the Spurs organization. As time went by, Tim Duncan enabled the transition of the team, to accommodate the strengths of the next generation of players, while continuing to mentor them. From 1997 to 2015, the Spurs had the highest win-percentage of all franchises in the four major sport leagues (NBA, NFL, NHL and MLB). In other words, they were the winning-est team in North America.[11] They had indeed become a dynasty.[12]

In June 2003, David Robinson walked out of the Spurs locker room after playing his last game. He was impeccably dressed, as always, in his designer suit, with his champagne-soaked game jersey in hand and adoring young son at his side. David accomplished what he had set out to do; he walked from the final game of his final season as a champion.[13]

Suggested Internet search:
David Robinson career highlights

ODE TO JOY

Ah, music! A magic beyond all we do here!

— *Albus Dumbledore*
J.K. Rowling

The Opening Ceremonies of the Olympic Games is when mankind comes together, in celebration of the human spirit. There is no competition; there are no winners, no losers. No awards are handed out. Rather, we all become children, enthusiastically cheering our individual teams, while simultaneously marveling at the diversity of our world.

Each Olympic Games is remembered not only for the accomplishment of the athletes, but also for the spectacle of the Opening Ceremonies. Who can forget the image of Muhammad Ali lighting the flame in Atlanta, with his indomitable spirit refusing to be curtailed by the shackles of Parkinson's disease; or the wheelchair-bound archer shooting a blazing arrow across the night sky in Barcelona to light the flame?[1]

When their turn came, the organizers of the 1998 Winter Olympics in Nagano, Japan organized something spectacular that, to this day, brings back goosebumps even to those who witnessed it only on television.

Their challenge was to come up with an idea that should be grandiose but not ostentatious, relatable to a wide audience but not commonplace, unique but not quirky, spectacular but not garish.

A live orchestra would perform—that, of course, had been done before. But not like this: the orchestra would be placed in five different continents. All of the five orchestras were to perform simultaneously, which would be shown live on a giant screen in the stadium. Even more—there would be thousands of singers inside the stadium also participating in the chorus. An audio-visual spectacle where seemingly the entirety of humankind comes together to perform.

This would be a logistical nightmare for the sound engineers. When audio-visual images are transmitted from different locations thousands of miles apart via satellites, there is a time delay of a couple of seconds. When the signals are put together, the symphony is thrown into a maddening cacophony. But these were Japanese engineers. They were more than capable of rising up to the challenge of mixing of the audio-visual feeds from all these sites, accommodating this time lag with such precision to make the orchestra sound seamless.[2]

The next challenge was to identify the appropriate song. The song had to match the magnitude of the vision, the grandeur of the setting, and the solemnity of the occasion. Friedrich Schiller's "Ode to Joy," immortalized by Beethoven as the grand finale of his Symphony No. 9, perhaps the greatest piece of music ever written (according to some music scholars and historians), was chosen.[3]

To better appreciate the selection of this song, one has to understand what it means to, and how it has impacted humanity around the world. It has stood as a beacon of hope, a bulwark against tyranny and oppression, a bonding of brotherhood.

When the Chinese students were protesting their totalitarian Government in Tiananmen Square in 1989, asking for more freedom, they played Beethoven's Symphony No. 9 over makeshift speakers. According to one of the protesters, "It gave us a sense of hope, solidarity...we are free at last..."[4]

In Chilé, when Augustine Pinochet had launched a bloody coup and had brutally imprisoned his opponents, the protesters stood outside the prison singing the "Himno de la Alegría"—"Ode to Joy." To the prisoners inside, locked up in their cells with just a grilled window through which the music could barely be heard, it symbolized hope even in the deepest, darkest hole.[5]

December 25, 1989 was the first Christmas that citizens of East and West Berlin were able to cross the border without any restrictions, as the Berlin Wall had been torn down. To commemorate the occasion, Leonard Bernstein conducted an orchestra with musicians drawn from East and West Berlin, UK, USA, Russia and France. There was a rousing rendering of Beethoven's Ninth with the word "freedom" substituted for "joy."[6]

No wonder, then, that the "Ode to Joy" was adopted as the Anthem of the European Union.

In Japan, every December, it is a tradition to perform and listen to Daiku, or Big Nine, as Beethoven's Symphony No. 9 is referred to. Entire concert halls are filled with enthusiastic citizens singing "Ode to Joy" in a karaoke style. In some performances, up to 5,000 people join in the chorus rendition, an almost spiritual experience for some members of the audience.[7]

Beethoven, arguably the greatest classical music composer that the world has ever seen, was one of the earliest artists to recognize the personal as political in a time of repression.[8]

According to Russell Steinberg, the Los Angeles-based composer-author-educator, "More than anyone, he defined the musician as an artist instead of as a servant. He felt that music was as elevated as philosophy—a search for truth and morality."[9]

In his Ninth Symphony, Beethoven was seen as offering a universal prayer—"All men will be brothers"—that was both hopeful prophecy and liberation battle cry.[10]

Seiji Osawa, the famous conductor from Japan, choreographed the orchestra from the Nagano Prefectural Cultural Hall. The orchestra had performers from 27 different countries. The performance started with Osawa waving his baton with a flourish.

As the orchestra started playing, one could feel the pulse rising within.

About a minute into the performance, a huge section of the audience had joined the chorus. A few seconds later, one could see the orchestras in the United Nations General Assembly Hall in New York City (America), at the Berlin Wall in Germany (Europe), False Bay near Cape Town, South Africa (Africa), the Forbidden City, China (Asia), and the Sydney Harbor (Australia), all performing in unison.[11]

The song had transcended all national, cultural, social, and religious barriers. It appeared that the entire world had come together to celebrate this moment of joy. The power of the human spirit was brought out in all its glory.

Schiller's immortal words rang true:

Ode to Joy

Joy, bright spark of divinity,
Daughter of Elysium,
Fire-inspired we tread
Thy sanctuary.
Thy magic power re-unites
All that custom has divided;
All men become brothers
Under the sway of thy gentle wings.[12]

Suggested Internet search:
1998 Olympics Ode to Joy

Acknowledgements

I can still remember sitting in my friend Sridhar's house, late at night, in the summer of 1980, watching McEnroe play Borg in the legendary Wimbledon final. His was the only house with a TV, so twenty of us were packed inside. That's how I got my first sports idol, John McEnroe. Most of my sports memories were formed at Sridhar's house, including the greatest day of my life (sorry, Priya) June 25, 1983, when India won their first Cricket World Cup.

I started writing these stories about one year ago, and I have pestered my friends and family to no end to get their opinions, mostly to help reassure me in my maiden attempt at writing. They have been kind enough to read, review, and offer suggestions. Thank you Aditya, Manasa, Sayuj, Shreyas, Sid, Pranav, Upasna, Sukanya, Shiva Athimber, Sumitra, Ashok, Vini, Ramesh, Shyam, Harini, Paul, Alan, and others.

I had no idea about sailing until Dr. Greg Boys, brilliant neuroradiologist and avid sailor, introduced me to the language of the high seas. I make no pretense about any prior knowledge of the subject. Any mistakes in *C'est La Vie* are completely mine. If the story even comes close to describing the thrills of sailing, the credit goes to Greg.

Thank you, Tony Bender, my friend from Ashley, North Dakota, who willingly gave me a tutorial in Publishing 101. And J Kay and Jason Minnix, for all of your support.

The most important gift that I've received from my teachers is the paradigm through which to view life. I'm thankful to everyone who helped to frame my perspective: my spiritual inspiration, Swami Chinmayananda; my Vedanta teachers, Hemuji and Swami Shivatmanandaji; and my literary icons, Kahlil Gibran and Kannadasan.

Thank you to Ms. Angela Gipple for proof-reading the book and cleaning up the mess created by a first-time author- especially those pesky punctuations. Thank you, Noel, for introducing me to Ms. Gipple.

Thank you, Priya, for everything. You have patiently tolerated your husband's maniacal sports addiction. Right from the time when I brought up the idea of this book, you have been its most ardent believer and supporter. I am so happy that you are with me.

Sankya, you've been the inspiration behind this book. I hope one day that you can realize the dream of seeing this book in an airport bookshop (the only place where we buy books). Thank you for putting up with the endless tales of the exploits of Tim Duncan, Tony Parker, Manu Ginobili, Steve Kerr, and Gregg Popovich. I'm sorry that your Appa does not know any other stories.

Tarika, my fiercest critic, ruthless editor. You've done a fantastic job designing, formatting, editing, and embellishing this book. I couldn't have done it without you.

Notes

The Champion Who Looked Back (Twice)

1. FitzSimons, Peter. "John Landy." *Great Australian Sports Champions*. Sydney, Australia: HarperSports, 2006. 225. Print.
2. Beard, Mary. "How Running Has Changed since the Four-minute Mile." *A Point of View*. BBC. 25 Apr. 2014. BBC. Web. 13 July 2015. Transcript.
3. Hirsch, George A. "BackTalk; Bannister's Milestone Recalls A Different Era in Sport." *New York Times* 25 Apr. 2004, US ed., Sports sec.: n. pag. *New York Times*. The New York Times Company. Web. 13 July 2015.
4. Bascomb, Neal. "The Perfect Mile." *The Perfect Mile: Three Athletes, One Goal, and Less than Four Minutes to Achieve It*. Boston: Houghton Mifflin, 2004. 229. Print.
5. Bascomb, Neal. "The Perfect Mile." *The Perfect Mile: Three Athletes, One Goal, and Less than Four Minutes to Achieve It*. Boston: Houghton Mifflin, 2004. 233-5. Print.
6. McCarthy, Michael. "Wake up Consumers? Nike's Brash CEO Dares to Just Do It." *USA Today* 16 June 2003, Advertising & Marketing sec.: n. pag. *USAToday*. Gannett Co. Inc., 16 June 2003. Web. 13 July 2015.
7. "Landy Admits He Ran In Final With Foot Injury." The Sydney Morning Herald (NSW : 1842 - 1954) 11 Aug 1954: 1. Web. 14 Jul 2015.
8. Bascomb, Neal. "The Perfect Mile." *The Perfect Mile: Three Athletes, One Goal, and Less than Four Minutes to Achieve It*. Boston: Houghton Mifflin, 2004. 254. Print.
9. Bascomb, Neal. "The Perfect Mile." *The Perfect Mile: Three Athletes, One Goal, and Less than Four Minutes to Achieve It*. Boston: Houghton Mifflin, 2004. 73. Print.

10. *Landy Assists Fallen Opponent - Still Wins Mile!* Australian Newsreel Item, 1956. *British Pathé.* British Pathé, 13 Apr. 2014. Web. 13 July 2015.
11. North, Sam. "Landy Took It All in His Stride and Is Still Making the Running." Sydney Morning Herald 1 May 2004, Sport sec.: n. pag.Sydney Morning Herald. The Sydney Morning Herald, 1 May 2004. Web. 13 July 2015.
12. Dunstan, Nick. "John Landy: A Significant Life." *Signs of the Times* Mar. 2006: n. pag. *Signs of the Times.* Signs of the Times & NetAdventist. Web. 13 July 2015.
13. *Landy Assists Fallen Opponent - Still Wins Mile!* Australian Newsreel Item, 1956. *British Pathé.* British Pathé, 13 Apr. 2014. Web. 13 July 2015.
14. FitzSimons, Peter. "John Landy." *Great Australian Sports Champions.* Sydney, Australia: HarperSports, 2006. 230. Print.
15. Gordon, Harry. "John Landy." *Athletics Australia.* Athletics Australia, 2004. Web. 13 July 2015.
16. " John Landy AC CVO MBE - Athletics." Sport Australia Hall of Fame. Sport Australia Hall of Fame, n.d. Web. 13 July 2015.

The Skyhook

1. *Kareem Abdul Jabbar: The Unstoppable Skyhook. Unscriptd.* Unscriptd, 10 June 2009. Web. 14 July 2015.
2. Adande, J.A. "Secrets of the Skyhook." *ESPN.* ESPN Internet Ventures, n.d. Web. 14 July 2015.
3. *Kareem Abdul Jabbar: The Unstoppable Skyhook. Unscriptd.* Unscriptd, 10 June 2009. Web. 14 July 2015.
4. Sokolove, Michael. "Clang!" *The New York Times Magazine.* The New York Times Company, 13 Feb. 2005. Web. 14 July 2015.
5. Johnson, Greg. "Chronicle of the Jam." NCAA News Archive. The National Collegiate Athletic Association, 2007. Web. 14 July 2015.
6. "Kareem Abdul-Jabbar Stats." *Sports Reference.* Sports Reference LLC, n.d. Web. 14 July 2015.

7. Sokolove, Michael. "Clang!" *The New York Times Magazine.* The New York Times Company, 13 Feb. 2005. Web. 14 July 2015.
8. Wooden, John, and Steve Jamison. *Wooden.* Chicago: Contemporary, 1997. 78. Print.
9. Smith, John Matthew. ""It's Not Really My Country": Lew Alcindor and the Revolt of the Black Athlete." *Journal of Sport History* 36.2 (2009): 223-44. *LA84.* LA84 Foundation. Web. 14 July 2015.
10. Johnson, Greg. "Chronicle of the Jam." NCAA News Archive. The National Collegiate Athletic Association, 2007. Web. 14 July 2015.
11. Sokolove, Michael. "Clang!" *The New York Times Magazine.* The New York Times Company, 13 Feb. 2005. Web. 14 July 2015.
12. *Kareem Abdul Jabbar: The Unstoppable Skyhook. Unscriptd.* Unscriptd, 10 June 2009. Web. 14 July 2015.
13. "Kareem Abdul-Jabbar Stats." *Sports Reference.* Sports Reference LLC, n.d. Web. 14 July 2015.
14. Doucette, Eddie. "Legendary Broadcaster of the Week: Eddie Doucette, Milwaukee Bucks." *NBA.* NBA Media Ventures LLC, 23 May 2007. Web. 14 July 2015.
15. "Kareem Abdul-Jabbar Stats." *Sports Reference.* Sports Reference LLC, n.d. Web. 14 July 2015.

Going Bananas

1. "Dani Alves Eats Banana in Response to Racist Taunt." *Yahoo Sports.* NBC Sports Network, 28 Apr. 2014. Web. 14 July 2015.
2. "Villareal - FC Barcelona: Comeback for Tito (2-3)." *FC Barcelona.* FC Barcelona, 27 Apr. 2014. Web. 14 July 2015.
3. "See Soccer Star's Reaction to Tossed Banana." *CNN.* Cable News Network, 28 Apr. 2014. Web. 14 July 2015.
4. "Milan's Boateng Takes Stand over Racism." *CNN.* Cable News Network, 4 Jan. 2013. Web. 14 July 2015.
5. Edwards, Luke. "AC Milan's Kevin-Prince Boateng Leads Team off Pitch in Protest at Racist Chanting in Friendly Match with Pro Patria." *The Telegraph.* Telegraph Media Group Ltd, 3 Jan. 2013. Web. 14 July 2015.

6. "Milan's Boateng Takes Stand over Racism." *CNN*. Cable News Network, 4 Jan. 2013. Web. 14 July 2015.

7. "Dani Alves Eats Banana in Response to Racist Taunt." *Yahoo Sports*. NBC Sports Network, 28 Apr. 2014. Web. 14 July 2015.

8. "Villareal - FC Barcelona: Comeback for Tito (2-3)." *FC Barcelona*. FC Barcelona, 27 Apr. 2014. Web. 14 July 2015.

9. Johnson, Reed. "Reaction by Daniel Alves to Taunt Draws World-Wide Cheers." *The Wall Street Journal*. Dow Jones & Company, Inc., 29 Apr. 2014. Web. 14 July 2015.

10. "#We Are All Monkeys: Balotelli, Suarez, Aguero Back Dani Alves' Banana-eating Anti-racism Campaign." *The Herald Scotland*. Herald & Times Group, 29 Apr. 2014. Web. 14 July 2015.

11. "Dani Alves Eats Banana in Response to Racist Taunt." *Yahoo Sports*. NBC Sports Network, 28 Apr. 2014. Web. 14 July 2015.

12. "Barcelona Star Dani Alves Calls Spain 'backward' on Racism after Banana Incident." *NY Daily News*. NY Daily News, 29 Apr. 2014. Web. 14 July 2015.

13. "Dani Alves Eats Banana in Response to Racist Taunt." *Yahoo Sports*. NBC Sports Network, 28 Apr. 2014. Web. 14 July 2015.

Bend, But Don't Break

1. Brill, Debbie, and James Lawton. "Eleven." *Jump*. Vancouver: Douglas & McIntyre, 1986. 172-73. Print.

2. "Bailey, Brill, Crothers, Joy and McKoy Honoured; Athletics Canada Inducts Inaugural Hall of Fame." *Athletics Canada*. Athletics Canada, 26 June 2011. Web. 14 July 2015.

3. Longman, Jeré. "An Olympian's Path Toward Inner Peace." *New York Times*. The New York Times Company, 27 Oct. 2008. Web. 14 July 2015.

4. Burnton, Simon. "50 Stunning Olympic Moments No30: Zola Budd's Rise and Fall in 1984." *The Guardian*. Guardian News and Media Ltd, 15 May 2012. Web. 14 July 2015.

5. Burnton, Simon. "50 Stunning Olympic Moments No30: Zola Budd's Rise and Fall in 1984." *The Guardian*. Guardian News and Media Ltd, 15 May 2012. Web. 14 July 2015.

6. Baker, Katie. "The Fall Heard 'Round the World." *The Daily Beast*. The Daily Beast Company LLC, 13 Aug. 2013. Web. 14 July 2015.

7. ""I Wish I'd Never Taken Part": Zola Budd on Her Olympic Games Regret." *Mirror*. Mirror Online, 21 May 2012. Web. 14 July 2015.

8. Burnton, Simon. "50 Stunning Olympic Moments No30: Zola Budd's Rise and Fall in 1984." *The Guardian*. Guardian News and Media Ltd, 15 May 2012. Web. 14 July 2015.

9. Budd, Zola. "Budd: 'My World Was Shattered'" *The Daily Mail* 13 Aug. 1984: n. pag. *The New York Times*. The New York Times Company. Web. 14 July 2015.

10. "Zola Budd Interview." *Gary Cohen Running*. N.p., Mar. 2014. Web. 14 July 2015.

11. Baker, Katie. "The Fall Heard 'Round the World." *The Daily Beast*. The Daily Beast Company LLC, 13 Aug. 2013. Web. 14 July 2015.

12. Burnton, Simon. "50 Stunning Olympic Moments No30: Zola Budd's Rise and Fall in 1984." *The Guardian*. Guardian News and Media Ltd, 15 May 2012. Web. 14 July 2015.

13. Burnton, Simon. "50 Stunning Olympic Moments No30: Zola Budd's Rise and Fall in 1984." *The Guardian*. Guardian News and Media Ltd, 15 May 2012. Web. 14 July 2015.

14. Wooldridge, Ian. "Zola Deserves Warm Welcome After All We Put Her Through." *Daily Mail*. Associated Newspapers Ltd., 9 Apr. 2003. Web. 14 July 2015.

15. "Brill, Schmidt Encourage Budd to 'learn and Grow'" *Ottawa Citizen* 17 Aug. 1984: 23. Print.

16. Brill, Debbie, and James Lawton. "Eleven." *Jump*. Vancouver: Douglas & McIntyre, 1986. Print.

17. Brill, Debbie, and James Lawton. "Eleven." *Jump*. Vancouver: Douglas & McIntyre, 1986. Print.

18. Brill, Debbie, and James Lawton. "Eleven." *Jump*. Vancouver: Douglas & McIntyre, 1986. 87-88. Print.

19. Brill, Debbie, and James Lawton. "Eleven." *Jump*. Vancouver: Douglas & McIntyre, 1986. 87-88. Print.
20. Brill, Debbie, and James Lawton. "Eleven." *Jump*. Vancouver: Douglas & McIntyre, 1986. 87-88. Print.
21. "Debbie Brill: Taking a Bad Day in Stride." *CBC Digital Archives*. CBC Radio-Canada, n.d. Web. 14 July 2015.
22. Brill, Debbie, and James Lawton. "Eleven." *Jump*. Vancouver: Douglas & McIntyre, 1986. Print.
23. Brill, Debbie, and James Lawton. "Eleven." *Jump*. Vancouver: Douglas & McIntyre, 1986. Print.
24. "Brill, Schmidt Encourage Budd to 'learn and Grow'" *Ottawa Citizen* 17 Aug. 1984: 23. Print.

Oh Say, Can You See

1. Berkow, Ira. "Sports of The Times; Proper Praise For Cheeks's Saving Grace." *New York Times* 11 May 2003: n. pag. *New York Times*. The New York Times Company. Web. 16 July 2015.
2. "2003 NBA Western Conference First Round Trail Blazers vs. Mavericks." *Basketball Reference*. Sports Reference LLC, n.d. Web. 16 July 2015.
3. "Recovering From An 0-3 Deficit." *NBA*. NBA Media Ventures LLC, 17 May 2007. Web. 16 July 2015.
4. Tokito, Mike. "Morning Jam: A Decade after Natalie Gilbert Assist, Maurice Cheeks Back in Head Coaching Ranks." *Oregon Live*. Oregon Live LLC, 11 Nov. 2013. Web. 16 July 2015.
5. Tokito, Mike. "Morning Jam: A Decade after Natalie Gilbert Assist, Maurice Cheeks Back in Head Coaching Ranks." *Oregon Live*. Oregon Live LLC, 11 Nov. 2013. Web. 16 July 2015.
6. Mayberry, Darnell. "Star-spangled Save: What Maurice Cheeks Did for Anthem Singer in Portland Is Still Remembered." *NewsOK*. NewsOK.com, 1 Nov. 2009. Web. 16 July 2015.
7. Tokito, Mike. "Morning Jam: A Decade after Natalie Gilbert Assist, Maurice Cheeks Back in Head Coaching Ranks." *Oregon Live*. Oregon Live LLC, 11 Nov. 2013. Web. 16 July 2015.
8. Tokito, Mike. "Morning Jam: A Decade after Natalie Gilbert Assist, Maurice Cheeks Back in Head Coaching

Ranks." *Oregon Live*. Oregon Live LLC, 11 Nov. 2013.
Web. 16 July 2015.

9. Tokito, Mike. "Morning Jam: A Decade after Natalie
    Gilbert Assist, Maurice Cheeks Back in Head Coaching
    Ranks." *Oregon Live*. Oregon Live LLC, 11 Nov. 2013.
    Web. 16 July 2015.
10. Smith, Sam. "76ers Coach Maurice Cheeks Still Handing
    out Assists." *Chicago Tribune*. Chicago Tribune, 14 Mar.
    2008. Web. 16 July 2015.
11. McGarr, Eliabeth. "Natalie Gilbert." *Sports Illustrated*.
    Time Inc., 2 Aug. 2010. Web. 16 July 2015.
12. "Maurice Cheeks." *Basketball Reference*. Sports
    Reference LLC, n.d. Web. 16 July 2015.
13. Berkow, Ira. "Sports of The Times; Proper Praise For
    Cheeks's Saving Grace." *New York Times* 11 May 2003:
    n. pag. *New York Times*. The New York Times Company.
    Web. 16 July 2015.
14. Berkow, Ira. "Sports of The Times; Proper Praise For
    Cheeks's Saving Grace." *New York Times* 11 May 2003:
    n. pag. *New York Times*. The New York Times Company.
    Web. 16 July 2015.

Natalie Gilbert's rendition of National Anthem and physical
reactions:

Tokito, Mike. "Morning Jam: A Decade after Natalie Gilbert
    Assist, Maurice Cheeks Back in Head Coaching
    Ranks." *Oregon Live*. Oregon Live LLC, 11 Nov. 2013.
    Web. 16 July 2015.

Ready, Shoot, Aim

1. "NBA & ABA Career Leaders and Records for 3-Pt Field
    Goal Pct." *Basketball Reference*. Sports Reference LLC,
    n.d. Web. 14 July 2015.
2. "NBA & ABA Career Leaders and Records for 3-Pt Field
    Goal Pct." *Basketball Reference*. Sports Reference LLC,
    n.d. Web. 14 July 2015.
3. "Kerr Caps Memorable Final." *NBA*. NBA Media Ventures
    LLC, n.d. Web. 14 July 2015.
4. "Kerr Caps Memorable Final." *NBA*. NBA Media Ventures
    LLC, n.d. Web. 14 July 2015.

5. Golliver, Ben. "Spurs Coach Gregg Popovich Profiled in Sports Illustrated, Whether He Likes It or Not." *Sports Illustrated*. Time Inc., 25 Apr. 2013. Web. 14 July 2015.
6. Golliver, Ben. "Spurs Coach Gregg Popovich Profiled in Sports Illustrated, Whether He Likes It or Not." *Sports Illustrated*. Time Inc., 25 Apr. 2013. Web. 14 July 2015.
7. Brown, Kirk. "How Does an NBA Basketball Player Spend a Workday?" *eHow*. Demand Media Inc., n.d. Web. 14 July 2015.
8. *San Antonio Spurs 2002-2003 NBA Champions*. Dir. Steve Michaud. Perf. Tim Duncan, David Robinson, Steve Kerr. Warner Brothers, 2003. DVD.
9. *San Antonio Spurs 2002-2003 NBA Champions*. Dir. Steve Michaud. Perf. Tim Duncan, David Robinson, Steve Kerr. Warner Brothers, 2003. DVD.
10. *San Antonio Spurs 2002-2003 NBA Champions*. Dir. Steve Michaud. Perf. Tim Duncan, David Robinson, Steve Kerr. Warner Brothers, 2003. DVD.
11. "Steve Kerr 2002-03 Game Log." *Basketball Reference*. Sports Reference LLC, n.d. Web. 14 July 2015.
12. *San Antonio Spurs 2002-2003 NBA Champions*. Dir. Steve Michaud. Perf. Tim Duncan, David Robinson, Steve Kerr. Warner Brothers, 2003. DVD.
13. *San Antonio Spurs 2002-2003 NBA Champions*. Dir. Steve Michaud. Perf. Tim Duncan, David Robinson, Steve Kerr. Warner Brothers, 2003. DVD.
Commentary from Game 6 2003 NBA Western Conference Finals:
San Antonio Spurs 2002-2003 NBA Champions. Dir. Steve Michaud. Perf. Tim Duncan, David Robinson, Steve Kerr. Warner Brothers, 2003. DVD.

The (Un)Spoiled Brat

1. Van Gilder Cooke, Sonia. "John McEnroe, 1981." *Time*. Time Inc., 18 June 2012. Web. 15 July 2015.
2. Schwartz, Larry. "McEnroe Was McNasty on and off the Court." *ESPN Classic*. ESPN Internet Ventures, n.d. Web. 15 July 2015.
3. Simons, Chris. "McEnroe's Petulant Outburst Leads to Painful Exit for Crying Child." *Independent.co.uk*. Independent.co.uk, 31 July 2000. Web. 15 July 2015.

4. Schwartz, Larry. "McEnroe Was McNasty on and off the Court." *ESPN Classic*. ESPN Internet Ventures, n.d. Web. 15 July 2015.
5. Touré. "John McEnroe's New Game." *Men's Journal* Sept. 2008: n. pag. *Men's Journal*. Men's Journal LLC. Web. 15 July 2015.
6. Dawidoff, Nicholas. "John McEnroe Is Still Pretty Complicated." *The New York Times Magazine*. The New York Times Company, 22 Aug. 2008. Web. 15 July 2015.
7. Hodgkinson, Mark, Simon Briggs, Brendan Gallager, and Ian Chadband. "Wimbledon: The 10 Greatest Moments." *The Telegraph*. Telegraph Media Group Ltd, 19 June 2011. Web. 15 July 2015.
8. Touré. "John McEnroe's New Game." *Men's Journal* Sept. 2008: n. pag. *Men's Journal*. Men's Journal LLC. Web. 15 July 2015.
9. "McEnroe Pays Tribute to Nelson Mandela." *ATP Champions Tour*. ATP Champions Tour, 7 Dec. 2013. Web. 15 July 2015.
10. Lapchick, Richard E. "A Legacy of Change and Hope." *ESPN*. ESPN Internet Ventures, 6 Feb. 2015. Web. 15 July 2015.
11. Ashe, Arthur, and Arnold Rampersad. *Days of Grace*. New York: Ballantine, 1993. 118-19. Print.
12. Zverina, Ivan. "South Africa Uses Big Bucks to Lure Stars." *Eugene Register-Guard* 12 Jan. 1984, sec. C: 2C. *UPI*. United Press International, Inc. Web. 15 July 2015.
13. Corrigall, Mary. *International Boycott of Apartheid Sport*. Issue brief. N.p.: United Nations Unit on Apartheid, n.d. *South African History Online*. South African History Online, 1971. Web. 15 July 2015.
14. Berkow, Ira. "Sports of the Times; the Protest of One Man." Editorial. *The New York Times* 1 Dec. 1988, Sports sec.: n. pag. *The New York Times*. The New York Times Company. Web. 15 July 2015.
15. "Prize Money and Finance." *Wimbledon*. IBM Corp. AELTC, n.d. Web. 15 July 2015.
16. Zverina, Ivan. "South Africa Uses Big Bucks to Lure Stars." *Eugene Register-Guard* 12 Jan. 1984, sec. C:

2C. *UPI.* United Press International, Inc. Web. 15 July 2015.

17. Ostler, Scot. "Money Sometimes Speaks Louder Than Morals In South Africa Sports." *Los Angeles Times* 10 Dec. 1987: n. pag. *Orlando Sentinel.* Orlando Sentinel. Web. 15 July 2015.

18. Touré. "John McEnroe's New Game." *Men's Journal* Sept. 2008: n. pag. *Men's Journal.* Men's Journal LLC. Web. 15 July 2015.

19. Touré. "John McEnroe's New Game." *Men's Journal* Sept. 2008: n. pag. *Men's Journal.* Men's Journal LLC. Web. 15 July 2015.

20. Touré. "John McEnroe's New Game." *Men's Journal* Sept. 2008: n. pag. *Men's Journal.* Men's Journal LLC. Web. 15 July 2015.

C'est La Vie

1. "Lemieux's Sportsmanship Still Recognized." *The Edmonton Journal* 13 Mar. 2008: n. pag. *Canada.com.* Postmedia Network, Inc. Web. 15 July 2015.

2. "Rules." *United States Sailing Association.* United States Sailing Association, n.d. Web. 15 July 2015.

3. Lacey, Hester. "Lawrence Lemieux, Canada." *Financial Times.* The Financial Times Ltd., 9 June 2012. Web. 15 July 2015.

4. Lacey, Hester. "Lawrence Lemieux, Canada." *Financial Times.* The Financial Times Ltd., 9 June 2012. Web. 15 July 2015.

5. "History of the Finn." *Finn Class.* International Finn Association, Inc., n.d. Web. 15 July 2015.

6. "Lawrence Lemieux Bio, Stats, and Results." *Sports Reference.* Sports Reference LLC, n.d. Web. 15 July 2015.

7. Heppell, Toby. "How to Start Faster." *Yachts & Yachting.* Chelsea Magazines Ltd., n.d. Web. 15 July 2015.

8. Private conversation with Greg Boys, MD

9. Lacey, Hester. "Lawrence Lemieux, Canada." *Financial Times.* The Financial Times Ltd., 9 June 2012. Web. 15 July 2015.

10. Lacey, Hester. "Lawrence Lemieux, Canada." *Financial Times*. The Financial Times Ltd., 9 June 2012. Web. 15 July 2015.

11. Lacey, Hester. "Lawrence Lemieux, Canada." *Financial Times*. The Financial Times Ltd., 9 June 2012. Web. 15 July 2015.

12. "Lemieux's Sportsmanship Still Recognized." *The Edmonton Journal* 13 Mar. 2008: n. pag. *Canada.com*. Postmedia Network, Inc. Web. 15 July 2015.

13. "Lemieux's Sportsmanship Still Recognized." *The Edmonton Journal* 13 Mar. 2008: n. pag. *Canada.com*. Postmedia Network, Inc. Web. 15 July 2015.

14. Lacey, Hester. "Lawrence Lemieux, Canada." *Financial Times*. The Financial Times Ltd., 9 June 2012. Web. 15 July 2015.

15. Private conversation with Greg Boys, MD

16. "The Seoul Games: Notes: Canadian Sailor Takes Time Out From Finn Race to Make Rescue." *Los Angeles Times* 26 Sept. 1988: n. pag. *Los Angeles Times*. Los Angeles Times. Web. 15 July 2015.

17. "20 Years Later, Seoul Sailor Still a Hero." *The Calgary Herald* 30 May 2008: n. pag. *Canada.com*. Postmedia Network, Inc. Web. 15 July 2015.

18. "Lemieux's Sportsmanship Still Recognized." *The Edmonton Journal* 13 Mar. 2008: n. pag. *Canada.com*. Postmedia Network, Inc. Web. 15 July 2015.

Attention to Details

1. "UCLA Bruins." *Basketball Reference*. Sports Reference LLC, n.d. Web. 17 July 2015.

2. Solorzano, Tony. "The Coach Was No Self Proclaimed Wizard." *Mid Valley Sports*. Mid Valley Sports, 13 June 2010. Web. 15 July 2015.

3. Walton, Bill. "Wooden Tribute." *BillWalton.com*. N.p., n.d. Web. 15 July 2015.

4. "Reactions to the Passing of Coach John Wooden." *UCLA Newsroom*. UCLA, 4 June 2010. Web. 18 Aug. 2015.

5. Wooden, John, and Steve Jamison. *Wooden*. Chicago: Contemporary, 1997. 52. Print.

6. Wooden, John, and Steve Jamison. *Wooden*. Chicago: Contemporary, 1997. 60-63. Print.

7. Luther, Claudia. "Coach John Wooden's Lesson on Shoes and Socks." *UCLA Newsroom*. UCLA, 4 June 2010. Web. 22 July 2015.
8. Wooden, John, and Steve Jamison. *Wooden*. Chicago: Contemporary, 1997. 60. Print.
9. Wooden, John, and Steve Jamison. *Wooden*. Chicago: Contemporary, 1997. 61. Print.
10. Luther, Claudia. "Coach John Wooden's Lesson on Shoes and Socks." *UCLA Newsroom*. UCLA, 4 June 2010. Web. 22 July 2015.
11. Wooden, John, and Steve Jamison. *Wooden*. Chicago: Contemporary, 1997. 61. Print.
12. Wooden, John, and Steve Jamison. *Wooden*. Chicago: Contemporary, 1997. 61-62. Print.
13. Wooden, John, and Steve Jamison. *Wooden*. Chicago: Contemporary, 1997. 60-63. Print.
14. Wooden, John, and Steve Jamison. *Wooden*. Chicago: Contemporary, 1997. 60. Print.

The Lovable Badass

1. "Metta World Peace Stats, Bio." *ESPN*. ESPN Internet Ventures, n.d. Web. 17 July 2015.
2. Burton, Roy. "10 Biggest Headcases in the NBA." *Bleacher Report*. Bleacher Report, Inc. Turner Broadcasting System, Inc., 28 Sept. 2012. Web. 17 July 2015.
3. Price, Satchel. "How 'Malice at the Palace' Changed the Careers of 6 Key Pacers." *SB Nation*. Vox Media, Inc., 19 Nov. 2014. Web. 17 July 2015.
4. "2003-04 Indiana Pacers Roster and Stats." *Basketball Reference*. Sports Reference LLC, n.d. Web. 17 July 2015.
5. "Indiana Pacers at Detroit Pistons Box Score, November 19, 2004." *Basketball Reference*. Sports Reference LLC, n.d. Web. 17 July 2015.
6. Pincus, David. "11/19/2004 - The Malice at the Palace." *SB Nation*. Vox Media, Inc., 18 Nov. 2010. Web. 17 July 2015.
7. Abrams, Jonathan. "The Malice at the Palace." *Grantland*. ESPN Internet Ventures, 20 Mar. 2012. Web. 17 July 2015.

8. Pincus, David. "11/19/2004 - The Malice at the Palace." *SB Nation*. Vox Media, Inc., 18 Nov. 2010. Web. 17 July 2015.

9. Pincus, David. "11/19/2004 - The Malice at the Palace." *SB Nation*. Vox Media, Inc., 18 Nov. 2010. Web. 17 July 2015.

10. Pincus, David. "11/19/2004 - The Malice at the Palace." *SB Nation*. Vox Media, Inc., 18 Nov. 2010. Web. 17 July 2015.

11. Abrams, Jonathan. "The Malice at the Palace." *Grantland*. ESPN Internet Ventures, 20 Mar. 2012. Web. 17 July 2015

12. McMenamin, Dave. "Ron Artest to Donate 2011-12 Salary." *ESPN*. ESPN Internet Ventures, 9 Dec. 2010. Web. 17 July 2015.

13. Medina, Mark. "Caught in the Web: Ron Artest to Receive Key to the City in Las Vegas." *Los Angeles Times*. Los Angeles Times, 12 Oct. 2010. Web. 17 July 2015.

14. "Lakers' Artest Receives Kennedy Citizenship Award." *NBA*. NBA Media Ventures LLC, 26 Apr. 2011. Web. 17 July 2015.

15. "Boston Celtics at Los Angeles Lakers Box Score, June 17, 2010." *Basketball Reference*. Sports Reference LLC, n.d. Web. 17 July 2015.

16. Solomon, Jerome. "Artest Was Game 7 MVP for Lakers." *Houston Chronicle*. Hearst Newspapers, LLC, 18 June 2010. Web. 17 July 2015.

17. Smith, Shelley. "Ron Artest: An Unlikely Advocate." *ESPN*. ESPN Internet Ventures, 19 Oct. 2010. Web. 17 July 2015.

18. Smith, Shelley. "Ron Artest: An Unlikely Advocate." *ESPN*. ESPN Internet Ventures, 19 Oct. 2010. Web. 17 July 2015.

19. Freeman, Eric. "Ron Artest Raffled off His Ring, Raised More than $500k." *Yahoo Sports*. Yahoo, 27 Dec. 2010. Web. 17 July 2015.

20. "About." *Xcel University*. Xcel University, n.d. Web. 17 July 2015.

21. Plaschke, Bill. "Ron Artest Turns out to Be a Mental Health Expert." *Los Angeles Times*. Los Angeles Times, 9 Sept. 2010. Web. 17 July 2015.

22. Plaschke, Bill. "Ron Artest Turns out to Be a Mental Health Expert." *Los Angeles Times*. Los Angeles Times, 9 Sept. 2010. Web. 17 July 2015.
23. Medina, Mark. "Ron Artest Explains Wanting to Change His Name to Metta World Peace." *Los Angeles Times*. Los Angeles Times, 29 June 2011. Web. 17 July 2015.
24. Medina, Mark. "Ron Artest Explains Wanting to Change His Name to Metta World Peace." *Los Angeles Times*. Los Angeles Times, 29 June 2011. Web. 17 July 2015.
25. "Lovable Badass in the Media." Web log post. *Lovable Badass*. Blogger, 1 Jan. 2011. Web. 17 July 2015.

A Goalkeeper in Midfield

1. Hackett, Robin. "Rene Higuita: El Loco." *ESPN FC*. ESPN Internet Ventures, 1 Dec. 2011. Web. 19 July 2015.
2. Hackett, Robin. "Rene Higuita: El Loco." *ESPN FC*. ESPN Internet Ventures, 1 Dec. 2011. Web. 19 July 2015.
3. "Soap Opera Pays Tribute to Colombia Football Legends." *Eurosport*. Yahoo, 2 Aug. 2013. Web. 19 July 2015.
4. Vickery, Tim. "The Legacy of Rene Higuita." *BBC*. BBC, 1 Feb. 2010. Web. 19 July 2015.
5. Hackett, Robin. "Rene Higuita: El Loco." *ESPN FC*. ESPN Internet Ventures, 1 Dec. 2011. Web. 19 July 2015.
6. "1990 FIFA World Cup Italy." *FIFA*. FIFA, n.d. Web. 19 July 2015.
7. "1990 FIFA World Cup Italy." *FIFA*. FIFA, n.d. Web. 19 July 2015.
8. "1990 FIFA World Cup Italy." *FIFA*. FIFA, n.d. Web. 19 July 2015.
9. "1990 FIFA World Cup Italy." *FIFA*. FIFA, n.d. Web. 19 July 2015.
10. "1990 FIFA World Cup Italy." *FIFA*. FIFA, n.d. Web. 19 July 2015.
11. Tynan, Gordon. "Higuita Sacked after Latest Drug Test Failure." *The Independent*. Independent.co.uk, 25 Nov. 2004. Web. 19 July 2015.

You Can't Measure Courage

1. Redmond, Derek. "Derek Redmond: The Day That Changed My Life." *Daily Mail.* Associated Newspapers Ltd, 27 July 2012. Web. 17 July 2015.
2. Redmond, Derek. "Derek Redmond: The Day That Changed My Life." *Daily Mail.* Associated Newspapers Ltd, 27 July 2012. Web. 17 July 2015.
3. "Derek Redmond Bio, Stats, and Results." *Sports Reference.* Sports Reference LLC, n.d. Web. 17 July 2015.
4. Burnton, Simon. "50 Stunning Olympic Moments No3: Derek Redmond and Dad Finish 400m." *The Guardian.* Guardian News and Media Ltd, 30 Nov. 2011. Web. 17 July 2015.
5. Burnton, Simon. "50 Stunning Olympic Moments No3: Derek Redmond and Dad Finish 400m." *The Guardian.* Guardian News and Media Ltd, 30 Nov. 2011. Web. 17 July 2015.
6. Burnton, Simon. "50 Stunning Olympic Moments No3: Derek Redmond and Dad Finish 400m." *The Guardian.* Guardian News and Media Ltd, 30 Nov. 2011. Web. 17 July 2015.
7. Redmond, Derek. "Derek Redmond: The Day That Changed My Life." *Daily Mail.* Associated Newspapers Ltd, 27 July 2012. Web. 17 July 2015.
8. Burnton, Simon. "50 Stunning Olympic Moments No3: Derek Redmond and Dad Finish 400m." *The Guardian.* Guardian News and Media Ltd, 30 Nov. 2011. Web. 17 July 2015.
9. Redmond, Derek. "Derek Redmond: The Day That Changed My Life." *Daily Mail.* Associated Newspapers Ltd, 27 July 2012. Web. 17 July 2015.
10. Redmond, Derek. "Derek Redmond: The Day That Changed My Life." *Daily Mail.* Associated Newspapers Ltd, 27 July 2012. Web. 17 July 2015.
11. Redmond, Derek. "Derek Redmond: The Day That Changed My Life." *Daily Mail.* Associated Newspapers Ltd, 27 July 2012. Web. 17 July 2015.
12. Burnton, Simon. "50 Stunning Olympic Moments No3: Derek Redmond and Dad Finish 400m." *The Guardian.*

Guardian News and Media Ltd, 30 Nov. 2011. Web. 17 July 2015.

13. "Jim Redmond to Carry Olympic Torch." *ESPN*. ESPN Internet Ventures, 10 Jan. 2012. Web. 17 July 2015.

14. Burnton, Simon. "50 Stunning Olympic Moments No3: Derek Redmond and Dad Finish 400m." *The Guardian*. Guardian News and Media Ltd, 30 Nov. 2011. Web. 17 July 2015.

15. Burnton, Simon. "50 Stunning Olympic Moments No3: Derek Redmond and Dad Finish 400m." *The Guardian*. Guardian News and Media Ltd, 30 Nov. 2011. Web. 17 July 2015.

16. Burnton, Simon. "50 Stunning Olympic Moments No3: Derek Redmond and Dad Finish 400m." *The Guardian*. Guardian News and Media Ltd, 30 Nov. 2011. Web. 17 July 2015.

17. Burnton, Simon. "50 Stunning Olympic Moments No3: Derek Redmond and Dad Finish 400m." *The Guardian*. Guardian News and Media Ltd, 30 Nov. 2011. Web. 17 July 2015.

18. Garfield, Bob. "Surprisingly, Humanity Wins over Scandal in Olympics Ads." *Advertising Age*. Crain Communications, Inc., 28 Feb. 2000. Web. 17 July 2015.

19. Redmond, Derek. "Derek Redmond: The Day That Changed My Life." *Daily Mail*. Associated Newspapers Ltd, 27 July 2012. Web. 17 July 2015.

20. Burnton, Simon. "50 Stunning Olympic Moments No3: Derek Redmond and Dad Finish 400m." *The Guardian*. Guardian News and Media Ltd, 30 Nov. 2011. Web. 17 July 2015.

21. "Derek Redmond Bio, Stats, and Results." *Sports Reference*. Sports Reference LLC, n.d. Web. 17 July 2015.

22. Burnton, Simon. "50 Stunning Olympic Moments No3: Derek Redmond and Dad Finish 400m." *The Guardian*. Guardian News and Media Ltd, 30 Nov. 2011. Web. 17 July 2015.

The Rear Admiral

1. "San Antonio Spurs History." *NBA*. NBA Media Ventures LLC, n.d. Web. 15 July 2015.
2. "David Robinson Career Stats." *NBA*. NBA Media Ventures LLC, n.d. Web. 15 July 2015.
3. "San Antonio Spurs History." *NBA*. NBA Media Ventures LLC, n.d. Web. 15 July 2015.
4. "David Robinson Career Stats." *NBA*. NBA Media Ventures LLC, n.d. Web. 15 July 2015.
5. "San Antonio Spurs History." *NBA*. NBA Media Ventures LLC, n.d. Web. 15 July 2015.
6. "San Antonio Spurs History." *NBA*. NBA Media Ventures LLC, n.d. Web. 15 July 2015.
7. "San Antonio Spurs History." *NBA*. NBA Media Ventures LLC, n.d. Web. 15 July 2015.
8. Firestone, Roy. "Up Close Special." *Up Close Special with David Robinson and Tim Duncan*. ESPN Classic. 23 Feb. 2012. Television.
9. "San Antonio Spurs History." *NBA*. NBA Media Ventures LLC, n.d. Web. 15 July 2015.
10. "David and Valerie Robinson's Donation Totals $9 Million." *NBA*. NBA Media Ventures LLC, n.d. Web. 15 July 2015.
11. "San Antonio Spurs, The Best Team in North America For the Last 15 Years." *Sportige*. Sportige, 15 Apr. 2012. Web. 16 July 2015.
12. Greenberg, Neil. "With Five NBA Titles in 15 Years, the Spurs Are a Dynasty." *The Washington Post*. N.p., 16 June 2014. Web. 15 July 2015.
13. *San Antonio Spurs 2002-2003 NBA Champions*. Dir. Steve Michaud. Perf. Tim Duncan, David Robinson, Steve Kerr. Warner Brothers, 2003. DVD.

Ode to Joy

1. Wolfman-Arent, Avi. "The Top 10 Opening Ceremonies in Summer Olympic History." *Bleacher Report*. Bleacher Report, Inc. Turner Broadcasting System, Inc., 27 July 2012. Web. 16 July 2015.
2. Strom, Stephanie. "The XVIII Winter Games: Opening Ceremonies; The Latest Sport? After a Worldwide Effort,

Synchronized Singing Gets In." *The New York Times* 7 Feb. 1998: n. pag. *The New York Times.* The New York Times Company. Web. 15 July 2015.

3. Service, Tom. "Symphony Guide: Beethoven's Ninth ('Choral')." *The Guardian.* Guardian News and Media Ltd, 9 Sept. 2014. Web. 16 July 2015.

4. "Following the Ninth, Documentary, Venice, CA." *FollowingtheNinth.com.* Battle Hymns Productions, LLC, 2014. Web. 15 July 2015.

5. "Following the Ninth, Documentary, Venice, CA." *FollowingtheNinth.com.* Battle Hymns Productions, LLC, 2014. Web. 15 July 2015.

6. "Upheaval in the East: Berlin; Near the Wall, Bernstein Leads an Ode to Freedom." *The New York Times* 26 Dec. 1989: n. pag. *The New York Times.* The New York Times Company. Web. 15 July 2015.

7. Weisman, Steven R. "Japan Sings Along With Beethoven." *The New York Times* 29 Dec. 1990: n. pag. *The New York Times.* The New York Times Company. Web. 15 July 2015.

8. Gold, Daniel M. "'Following the Ninth' Explores Beethoven's Legacy." *The New York Times.* The New York Times Company, 31 Oct. 2013. Web. 15 July 2015.

9. Scher, Valerie. "Ode to Ludwig: Beethoven's Greatness Plays across Time." *MarketingCrossing.* MarketingCrossing, n.d. Web. 15 July 2015.

10. Gold, Daniel M. "'Following the Ninth' Explores Beethoven's Legacy." *The New York Times.* The New York Times Company, 31 Oct. 2013. Web. 15 July 2015.

11. Paquette, Jessica. "The Top 10 Opening Ceremonies in Winter Olympics History." *Bleacher Report.* Bleacher Report, Inc. Turner Broadcasting System, Inc., 6 Feb. 2014. Web. 16 July 2015.

12. "Prelude to Olympic Glory: Beethoven's "Ode to Joy"" *WGBH.* WGBH, n.d. Web. 15 July 2015.

Made in the USA
Charleston, SC
03 March 2017